CONSEQUENTIALISM

Consequentialism is the view that the rightness or wrongness of actions depends largely on their consequences. It is one of the most influential, and controversial, of all ethical theories. In this book, Julia Driver introduces and critically assesses consequentialism in all its forms.

After a brief historical introduction to the problem, Driver examines utilitarianism, and the arguments of its most famous exponents, John Stuart Mill and Jeremy Bentham, and explains the fundamental questions underlying utilitarian theory: what value is to be specified and how it is to be maximized.

Driver also discusses indirect forms of consequentialism, the important theories of motive-consequentialism and virtue-consequentialism, and explains why the distinction between subjective and objective consequentialism is so important. A central feature of the book is also a comparison of consequentialism with other influential ethical theories, particularly virtue ethics and the role of character.

Including helpful features such as glossary, chapter summaries, and annotated further reading at the end of each chapter, Consequentialism is ideal for students seeking an authoritative and clearly explained survey of this important problem.

Julia Driver is Professor of Philosophy at Washington University in St. Louis, USA. She is the author of Uneasy Virtue (2001) and Ethics: The Fundamentals (2006), and is co-editor of the Journal of Ethics and Social Philosophy, as well as co-editor of the Normative Ethics section of The Stanford Encyclopedia of Philosophy.

New Problems of Philosophy
Series Editor: *José Luis Bermúdez*

The New Problems of Philosophy series provides accessible and engaging surveys of the most important problems in contemporary philosophy. Each book examines either a topic or theme that has emerged on the philosophical landscape in recent years, or a longstanding problem refreshed in light of recent work in philosophy and related disciplines. Clearly explaining the nature of the problem at hand and assessing attempts to answer it, books in the series are excellent starting points for undergraduate and graduate students wishing to study a single topic in depth. They will also be essential reading for professional philosophers. Additional features include chapter summaries, further reading and a glossary of technical terms.

CONSEQUENTIALISM

Julia Driver

Routledge
Taylor & Francis Group

LONDON AND NEW YORK

First published 2012
by Routledge
2 Park Square, Milton Park, Abingdon, Oxon, OX14 4RN

Simultaneously published in the USA and Canada
by Routledge
711 Third Ave., 8th Floor, New York, NY. 10017

Routledge is an imprint of the Taylor & Francis Group, an informa business

British Library Cataloguing in Publication Data
A catalogue record for this book is available from the British Library

Library of Congress Cataloging in Publication Data
Driver, Julia, 1961-
Consequentialism / by Julia Driver.
    p. cm. -- (New problems of philosophy) Includes bibliographical references
    (p.) and index. 1. Consequentialism (Ethics) I. Title.
    BJ1500.C63D75 2011   171'.5--dc23
    2011024310

ISBN: 978-0-415-77257-0 (hbk)
ISBN: 978-0-415-77258-7 (pbk)
ISBN: 978-0-203-14925-6 (ebk)

Typeset in Joanna and Scala Sans by
Bookcraft Ltd, Stroud, Gloucestershire

Printed and bound in Great Britain by
CPI Antony Rowe, Chippenham, Wiltshire

CONTENTS

ACKNOWLEDGEMENTS

I owe a great deal of thanks to many people over the years for discussing the ideas in this book. These conversations have helped me to sharpen my position on consequentialism. I particularly would like to thank David Brink, Eric Brown, Sarah Buss, Roger Crisp, Jamie Dreier, Brad Hooker, Tom Hurka, Elinor Mason, Alastair Norcross, Philip Pettit, Peter Railton, Connie Rosati, Walter Sinnott-Armstrong, Michael Slote, Michael Smith, Roy Sorensen, Peter Vallentyne, Mark van Roojen, Eric Wiland, and Susan Wolf. Support for work on the manuscript was provided by a Fellowship from the National Endowment for the Humanities, in 2004/5, and I am deeply grateful to the Endowment for the support.

Some material in this book has been presented at the tenth meeting of the International Society for Utilitarian Studies held in Berkeley, California at the Kadish School of Law, the University of Toronto, the University of Missouri, Columbia, the University of Wyoming, the Political Theory workshop at Washington University in St. Louis, and at the second annual Workshop on Normative Ethics at the University of Arizona. I thank the members of those audiences for their very helpful discussions.

I would also like to thank the three anonymous reviewers for Routledge, who provided excellent feedback on the manuscript. Their comments went far beyond the norm and I'm grateful for the care they took in assessing the manuscript and making constructive comments.

Thanks are owed to Sam Means, one of my Presidential Scholars when I taught at Dartmouth, for his help in hunting down library materials and his insights from the undergraduate point of view about what seems odd (as well as persuasive!) about consequentialism. I would also like to thank the students in my graduate seminar on consequentialism at Washington University in St. Louis for their very active class discussion: Nate Adams, Nicholas Baima, Lauren Olin, Tyler Paytas, Felipe Romero, Bryan Stagner, Martin Turner, MaryEllen VanDerHayden, and David Winchell. The discussion pushed me to work harder on clarifying my final position.

Portions of Chapter 1 have appeared in the entry "History of Utilitarianism," in *The Stanford Encyclopedia of Philosophy*; and portions of Chapter 6 in "The 'Actual' in 'Actualism'," in *Mind, Ethics, and Conditionals*, ed. Ian Ravenscroft (New York: Oxford University Press, 2009). I thank Oxford University Press for permission to reprint this material.

INTRODUCTION

Moral evaluation is central to the critical practices of human beings. In order for us to navigate the world successfully, we need to be able to make normative judgments about what is good and bad, and, particularly, what sorts of behaviors and ways of life are morally good and morally bad. Throughout the history of philosophy a variety of different types of theory have been suggested and developed as a way of understanding moral practice. The topic of this book is one of these theories – consequentialism.

Consequentialism is a view in moral philosophy that, on first blush, many find intuitively plausible. Roughly, it is the view that the moral quality of action and character is determined by the *effects* of the action or character trait (relative to the agent's options). The view has a *prima facie* plausibility, at least, due to the fact that very many people consider the consequences of alternative courses of action before making a decision about what to do. Suppose that Alice has decided to give some money to charity, and is trying to decide which charity to contribute to. At least one factor in her deliberations will be how effective her contribution would be. She is likely to favor the charity that spends its money most effectively. If so, she is weighing the effects of the contribution in making her decision.

Where consequentialism departs from this model, however, it becomes more controversial. The consequentialist not only holds that effects are morally relevant; the consequentialist also holds that effects are *all* that is morally relevant. For example, producing the best effects is necessary and sufficient for an action's rightness on this view, not simply necessary.

This general characterization is rather vague. We will initially be looking closely at a version of consequentialism, utilitarianism, which holds that the right action *maximizes* the good. Utilitarianism is probably the best-known version of consequentialism, but it is certainly not the only version. Egoism also counts as a form of consequentialism, but the egoist holds that the only good that needs to be produced is the good of the individual performing the action. Thus, egoism holds a partial, as opposed to impartial, standard.

There are fundamentally two parts to a consequentialist approach to moral evaluation: the value one identifies as fundamental, and the proper approach to the value. Consider the example of the evaluation of 'right action'. Classical utilitarianism holds that the right action is the action that maximizes the good, and that good is fundamentally a matter of pleasure and/or pain avoidance. Here, the fundamental value is pleasure and the approach to value is maximization.

The book falls into two main parts: the first four chapters provide an overview of consequentialism in the literature. It is not an exhaustive overview, but it will give a fairly good representation of the different positions. Chapters 5 to 7 develop my own, rather idiosyncratic theory. In defending the approach I take, however, I discuss the alternatives.

Chapter 1 goes over some of the history of this approach to moral philosophy. The basic insight that the theory trades on has been recognized as long as people have been thinking about ethics – namely the insight that the effects of what one does are morally significant and should factor into moral evaluation. However, the theory didn't begin to be systematically developed until the classical utilitarians – Jeremy Bentham and John Stuart Mill – in the eighteenth and nineteenth centuries. Chapter 1 explores the precursors to Bentham and Mill.

Chapter 2 focuses on developing the two distinct portions of the theory, value and the approach to value. Different theories of value are critically discussed. The main difference lies in the split between theories that identify value in subjective states, such as pleasure and desire, and theories that build in something objective, such as actual accomplishment, that may contribute to the agent's life regardless of whether the agent experiences positive subjective states due to the accomplishment.

Different approaches to value are contrasted with the classic maximization of value approach favored by utilitarians. In particular, the view that satisficing the good is what really sets the standard for 'right action' is critically evaluated. This approach was intended to solve the problem of demandingness – maximization of the good makes our moral requirements very demanding indeed. However, there are considerable problems with the satisficing approach, the main one being that, when properly spelled out, it seems to make requirements irrational.

In Chapter 3 the issue of how to aggregate the good is explored. In the initial, classical formulation of the theory it was left open as to whether we are obliged to maximize total good or average good. There is considerable practical difference between the two options. If one opts for total good, then one may be in a position of favoring an outcome in which an extremely large number of people are living lives barely worth living, as opposed to an outcome in which fewer people live much better lives. This is strongly counterintuitive. If one opts for average utility, on the other hand, one may end up favoring an outcome in which it is wrong to add to a population of fairly happy people additional people who are only very slightly less happy. And this seems highly counterintuitive as well. These options are critically discussed in more detail, as are other approaches to aggregation. Also considered is the issue of whether to include the well-being of future people in the aggregation.

Act-consequentialism, which holds that the right action is the action that itself has the best overall effects among the options available to the agent, has been subject to numerous counterexamples. One such example tries to show that the theory gives us the wrong answer when there is a conflict between maximizing utility and, for example, doing what is just. It may be that a sheriff can save innocent lives by sacrificing an innocent man to avoid a riot – but that would be the wrong thing to do, since that action is unjust. Very many consequentialists, however, do not think that this example warrants giving up the theory altogether. Rather, they suggest, the theory should be modified so that actions are evaluated not according to their own direct effects but, instead, to the effects of something else, such as a rule. This maneuver is the indirection strategy, and rule-consequentialism is the main form of the theory that employs this strategy. In Chapter 4 the indirection strategy is explored, focusing primarily on a critical discussion of rule-consequentialism.

Another issue that has come up in the further development of consequentialism is the split between objective consequentialists, who regard the right action as the one that produces the best actual results amongst the alternatives open to the agent, and subjective consequentialism, which holds that the right action is the one that produces the best expected effects among the options open to the agent. In Chapter 5 I present the alternatives, and argue in favor of the objective standard of 'right'. Both views are critically discussed and this involves a review of the considerations that lead writers to adopt subjective consequentialism in favor of objective consequentialism. One of the most significant has to do with worries about moral luck: the objective view seems to condemn actions that produce bad results, even though the agent did not foresee those bad results, and, on the most extreme form of the theory, even when the agent could not reasonably have foreseen those results. This seems problematic, but becomes much less so when a distinction between 'right and wrong' and 'praiseworthy and blameworthy' is noted. By failing to meet the objective standard, one may have performed the wrong action, for example, but that does not make one blameworthy.

One issue left potentially unresolved in Chapter 5 is whether objective consequentialism can say anything at all about action guidance. Since the view defended offers a standard for evaluation, rather than a decision-procedure from which a standard can be extracted, this is an interesting issue. Earlier writers, such as Peter Railton, have suggested that recommended decision-procedures turn out to be an empirical issue. This is true, though given some basic empirical assumptions we can offer some views on how people ought to go about making moral decisions, and what factors should be considered. In Chapter 6 this issue is explored in more detail, with the primary focus on the debate between possibilists and actualists. Should Mary agree to do something that if she does it would be great, but that she also thinks she is very unlikely to do? Further, if she fails to do it, would it be very bad, much worse than any of the alternatives open to her that she is likely to follow? The possibilist says "yes" – after all, she can do it. The actualist says "no" – since she is very unlikely to do it, and failure to do it is worse than the alternatives she is likely to pursue. These options are discussed, and I argue in favor of the actualist position.

In the last chapter, Chapter 7, I expand on my positive theory by discussing global consequentialism, contrasting my approach with the approach of others who have written on this in the past. The final version of the theory is contextual, objective, and global – judgments of 'right' in everyday discourse are evaluated relative to a context with a built-in contrast (though there is still a fact of the matter as to what is, all things considered, 'right'); the standard is objective; and the standard can be applied to any feature relevant to agency, such as intentions, motives, disposition, and actions. Problems with this approach are discussed, and the approach defended.

1

BACKGROUND AND HISTORY

In moral philosophy consequentialism is the view that the moral quality of an action – for example, the *rightness* of the action – is completely determined by the action's consequences, relative to the consequences of alternative actions open to the agent. The core idea captured by this approach has a good deal of intuitive appeal. One of the things, at least, that we look for when evaluating actions morally is their effects. Further, most consequentialists are committed to the view that we ought to *maximize* the good effects. The idea is that producing more good is better than producing less. Of course, people often follow rules of thumb to guide them through the normal, day-to-day decisions they make about what to do. But sometimes people are confronted with situations that call for careful thought about what they should – morally – do. For example, suppose that Maria has decided to give some money to charity. A consequentialist would hold that she should give the money to the charity that will have the best overall impact in promoting happiness, or well-being, relative to the available alternatives, given what Maria knows about the charities. If she has good evidence, for example, that Oxfam has a greater positive impact than the others, then that's the charity she should give to. While in cases like this the view seems quite intuitively plausible, there will be situations in which a commitment to maximizing the well-being of others seems morally counterintuitive, since it may conflict with our intuitions about justice and basic human rights. This will be explored in depth later in the book.

More generally the view can be applied to other things that we evaluate morally – such as rules, policies, motives, and dispositions. Many early theories of moral evaluation incorporated the insight that effects of actions were *relevant* to the moral evaluation of the actions. But this isn't fully consequentialist. Consequentialists hold that the moral quality of a person's actions, or character, is *solely* determined by the effects of the action or character trait in question. Usually the effects, that is the good to be brought about, are understood in terms of happiness or well-being. In this way, some have argued that Epicurus was an early consequentialist due to his development of hedonism. He, like Jeremy Bentham later, believed that the good was pleasure and the bad was pain. Thus, we should seek to achieve pleasure and avoid pain, if we would like to live a good life. Epicurus limits the scope of the relevant consequences to the self, so he is generally regarded as articulating the brand of consequentialism that is called egoism – one should promote the good, but this is understood as what is good for the *self*, not good overall.[1] Egoism is not taken as seriously today, mainly because the task of reconciling our moral intuitions regarding what we ought to do with what promotes individual self-interest does not seem likely to succeed. In this volume we will be focusing on the form of consequentialism most identified with utilitarianism, and which holds that the scope of the relevant consequences is extended to include the happiness, or well-being, of *others*.

Another candidate for early consequentialist is the early Chinese philosopher Mo-Tzu. Geoffrey Scarre, and others, note that Mo-Tzu (fl. c. 420 BC) was a consequentialist in that he often criticized customs by noticing their uselessness or actual harmfulness.[2] What was wanting was universal love, or benevolence:

> When nobody in the world loves any other, naturally the strong will overpower the weak, the many will oppress the few, the wealthy will mock the poor, those honored will disdain the humble, the cunning will deceive the simple. Therefore all the calamities, strife, complaints, and hatred in the world have arisen out of want of universal love. Therefore humanists disapprove of this want.[3]

Further, he noted that effects matter to the moral quality of an action or policy. Like the later utilitarians, Bentham and Mill, Mo-Tzu seemed motivated to promote social reform. His view that universal benevolence is what is needed to morally improve the world is echoed by Francis Hutcheson's views that virtue, at its root, is benevolence. Unfortunately, little work has been done on this interesting figure and what his influence might have been in the history of ethical theory.

Consequentialism in its modern form and in the Western tradition was heavily influenced by early sentimentalists, such as the 3rd Earl of Shaftesbury, Francis Hutcheson, and David Hume. Sentimentalism is, very broadly, the view that morality is a matter of feeling rather than reason, and it is usually opposed to rationalism, which holds that people can be motivated purely by reason to act on moral norms. Rationalism is perfectly compatible with utilitarianism, though most rationalists just as a matter of historical contingency happen to reject it. The work of the sentimentalists influenced the development of the most prominent form of consequentialism, classical utilitarianism. In this chapter, then, we will focus on drawing out the history of consequentialism from the British Moralists through G. E. Moore, who was writing on utilitarianism at the turn of the twentieth century.

1.1 Precursors of the classical approach

Though the first systematic account of utilitarianism was developed by Jeremy Bentham (1748–1832), the core insight motivating the theory occurred much earlier. That insight is that morally appropriate behavior will not harm others, but instead increase happiness or 'utility'. What is distinctive about utilitarianism is its approach in taking that insight and developing an account of moral evaluation and moral direction that expands on it. Early precursors of the classical utilitarians include the British Moralists, Cumberland, Shaftesbury, Hutcheson, Gay, and Hume. Of these, Francis Hutcheson (1694–1746) is explicitly utilitarian when it comes to action choice.

Some of the earliest utilitarian thinkers were the 'theological' utilitarians such as Richard Cumberland (1631–1718) and John Gay (1699–1745). They believed that promoting human happiness was incumbent on us since it was approved by God. After enumerating the ways in which humans come under obligations (by perceiving the "natural consequences of things," the obligation to be virtuous, our civil obligations that arise from laws, and obligations arising from "the authority of God") John Gay writes: "from the consideration of these four sorts of obligation ... it is evident that a full and complete obligation which will extend to all cases, can only be that arising from the authority of God; because God only can in all cases make a man happy or miserable: and therefore, since we are always obliged to that conformity called virtue, it is evident that the immediate rule or criterion of it is the will of God."[4] Gay held that since God wants the happiness of mankind, and since God's will gives us the criterion of virtue, "the happiness of mankind may be said to be the criterion of virtue, but once removed" (413). This view was combined with a view of human motivation with egoistic elements. A person's individual salvation, her eternal happiness, depended on conformity to God's will, as did virtue itself. Promoting human happiness and one's own coincided, but, given God's design, it was not an accidental coincidence.

This approach to utilitarianism, however, is not theoretically clean in the sense that it isn't clear what essential work God does, at least in terms of normative ethics. God as the source of normativity is compatible with utilitarianism, but utilitarianism doesn't require this.

Gay's influence on later writers, such as Hume, deserves note. It is in Gay's essay that some of the questions that concerned Hume on the nature of virtue are addressed. For example, Gay was curious about how to explain our practice of approbation and disapprobation of action and character. When we see an act that is vicious we disapprove of it. Further, we associate certain things with their effects, so that we form positive associations and negative associations that also underwrite our moral judgments. Of course, that we view happiness, including the happiness of others, as a good, is due to God's design. This is a feature crucial to the theological approach, which would clearly be rejected by Hume in favor of a naturalistic view of human nature and a reliance on our sympathetic engagement with others, an approach anticipated by Shaftesbury (see below). The theological approach to utilitarianism would be developed later by William Paley, for example, but the lack of any theoretical necessity in appealing to God would result in its diminishing appeal.

Anthony Ashley Cooper, the 3rd Earl of Shaftesbury (1671–1713), is generally thought to have been one of the earliest 'moral sense' theorists, holding that we possess a kind of 'inner eye' that allows us to make moral discriminations. This seems to have been an innate sense of right and wrong, or moral beauty and deformity. Again, aspects of this doctrine would be picked up by Francis Hutcheson and David Hume (1711–76). Hume, of course, would clearly reject any *robust* realist implications.[5] If the moral sense is like the other perceptual senses and enables us to pick up on properties out there in the universe around us, properties that exist independently of our perception of them, that are objective, then Hume clearly was not a moral sense theorist in this regard. But perception picks up on features of our environment that one could regard as having a contingent quality. There is one famous passage where Hume likens moral discrimination to the perception of secondary qualities, such as color. In modern terminology, these are response-dependent properties, and lack objectivity in the sense that they do not exist independently of our responses. This is radical. If an act is vicious, its viciousness is a matter of the human response (given a corrected perspective) to the act (or its perceived effects) and thus has a kind of contingency that seems unsettling, certainly unsettling to those who opted for the theological option.

So, the view that it is part of our very nature to make moral discriminations is very much in Hume. Further – and what is relevant to the development of utilitarianism – Shaftesbury's view that the virtuous person contributes to the good of the whole would figure into Hume's writings, though modified. It is the virtue that contributes to the good of the whole system, in the case of Hume's artificial virtues.

Shaftesbury held that in judging someone virtuous or good in a moral sense we need to perceive that person's impact on the systems of which he or she is a part. Here it sometimes becomes difficult to disentangle egoistic versus utilitarian lines of thought in Shaftesbury. He clearly states that whatever guiding force there is has made nature such that it is "the private interest and good of every one, to work towards the general good, which if a creature ceases to promote, he is actually so far wanting to himself, and ceases to promote his own happiness and welfare".[6] It is hard, sometimes, to discern the direction of the 'because'. If one should act to help others because it supports a system in which one's own happiness is more likely, then it looks really like a form of egoism. If one should help others because that's the right thing to do – and, fortunately, it also ends up promoting one's own interests – then that's more like utilitarianism, since the promotion of self-interest is a welcome effect but not what, all by itself, justifies one's character or actions.

Further, to be virtuous a person must have certain psychological capacities – they must be able to reflect on character, for example, and represent to themselves the qualities in others that are either approved or disapproved of.

> [I]n this case alone it is we call any creature worthy or virtuous when it can have the notion of a public interest, and can attain the speculation or science of what is morally good or ill, admirable or blamable, right or

> wrong ... we never say of ... any mere beast, idiot, or changeling, though ever so good-natured, that he is worthy or virtuous.[7]

Thus, animals are not objects of moral appraisal on this view, since they lack the necessary reflective capacities. Animals also lack the capacity for moral discrimination and would therefore seem to lack the moral sense. This raises some interesting questions. It would seem that the moral sense is a perception that something is the case. So it isn't merely a discriminatory sense that allows us to sort perceptions. It also has a propositional aspect, so that animals, which are not lacking in other senses, are lacking in this one.

The virtuous person is one whose affections, motives, dispositions are of the right sort, not one whose behavior is simply of the right sort and who is able to reflect on goodness, and her own goodness.[8] Similarly, the vicious person is one who exemplifies the wrong sorts of mental states, affections, and so forth. A person who harms others through no fault of his own "because he has convulsive fits which make him strike and wound such as approach him" is not vicious since he has no desire to harm anyone and his bodily movements in this case are beyond his control.[9]

Shaftesbury approached moral evaluation via the virtues and vices. His utilitarian leanings are distinct from his moral sense approach, and his overall sentimentalism. However, this approach highlights the move away from egoistic views of human nature – a trend picked up by Hutcheson and Hume, and later adopted by Mill in criticism of Bentham's version of utilitarianism. For writers like Shaftesbury and Hutcheson the main contrast was with egoism rather than rationalism.

Like Shaftesbury, Francis Hutcheson was much interested in virtue evaluation. He also adopted the moral sense approach. However, in his writings we also see an emphasis on action choice and the importance of moral deliberation to action choice. Hutcheson, in *An Inquiry Concerning Moral Good and Evil*, fairly explicitly spelled out a utilitarian principle of action choice.[10]

> In comparing the moral qualities of actions ... we are led by our moral sense of virtue to judge thus; that in equal degrees of happiness, expected to proceed from the action, the virtue is in proportion to the number of persons to whom the happiness shall extend (and here the dignity, or moral importance of persons, may compensate numbers); and, in equal numbers, the virtue is the quantity of the happiness, or natural good; or that the virtue is in a compound ratio of the quantity of good, and number

of enjoyers ... so that that action is best, which procures the greatest happiness for the greatest numbers; and that worst, which, in like manner, occasions misery.[11]

Scarre notes that some hold the moral sense approach incompatible with this emphasis on the use of reason to determine what we ought to do; there is an opposition between just apprehending what's morally significant and a model in which we need to reason to figure out what morality demands of us. But Scarre notes these are not actually incompatible:

> The picture which emerges from Hutcheson's discussion is of a division of labor, in which the moral sense causes us to look with favor on actions which benefit others and disfavor those which harm them, while consequentialist reasoning determines a more precise ranking order of practical options in given situations.[12]

The moral sense provides an account both of moral motivation and moral epistemology in that approval indicates moral goodness. Hutcheson is at great pains to distinguish moral from natural goodness. Something is naturally good when it is good, and yet does not exemplify agency. We like things that are naturally good – things like lovely weather and ice cream. But lovely weather and ice cream are not examples of moral goods. In the case of moral goods, we approve in addition to like. Ice cream is not a moral good, but when Alice gives Ann ice cream, knowing she would enjoy it, the act of giving is morally good. Further, if someone accidentally and non-negligently harms another, that is unfortunate, but not morally bad since the person's agency wasn't behind the bodily movement in the right way. If someone accidentally trips and steps on my foot I do not resent the person, though I would resent him if I thought he did it on purpose.

Scarre then uses the example of telling a lie to illustrate how the moral sense and the use of consequentialist reasoning are supposed to work for Hutcheson: lying is harmful to the person to whom one lies, and so this is viewed with disfavor, in general. However, in a specific case, if a lie is necessary to achieve some notable good, consequentialist reasoning will lead us to favor the lying. But this example seems to put all the emphasis on a consideration of consequences in moral approval and disapproval. Stephen Darwall notes that the moral sense is concerned with motives – we approve, for example, of the motive of benevolence, and the wider the scope the better. It is the motives rather than the consequences that are the objects of approval and disapproval. But inasmuch as the morally good person cares about what happens to others, and of course she will, she will rank acts in terms of their effects on others, and reason is used in calculating effects. So there is no incompatibility at all.[13]

Hutcheson was committed to maximization, it seems. However, he insisted on a caveat – that "the dignity or moral importance of persons may compensate numbers." One interpretation of this clause is to hold that he has added a deontological constraint – that we have a duty to others in virtue of their personhood to accord them fundamental dignity regardless of the numbers of others whose happiness is to be affected by the action in question.

Hume was heavily influenced by Hutcheson, who was one of his teachers. His system also incorporates insights from Shaftesbury, though he certainly lacks Shaftesbury's confidence that virtue is its own reward. In terms of his place in the history of utilitarianism we should note two distinct effects his system had. First, his account of the social utility of the artificial virtues influenced Bentham's thought on utility. Second, his account of the role sentiment played in moral judgment and commitment to moral norms influenced Mill's thoughts about the internal sanctions of morality. Mill would diverge from Bentham in developing the 'altruistic' approach to utilitarianism (which is actually a misnomer, but more on that later). Bentham, in contrast to Mill, represented the egoistic branch – his theory of human nature reflected Hobbesian psychological egoism.

1.2 The classical approach

The classical utilitarians, Bentham and Mill, were concerned with legal and social reform. If anything could be identified as the fundamental motivation behind the development of classical utilitarianism it would be the desire to see useless, corrupt laws and social practices changed. Accomplishing this goal required a normative ethical theory employed as a critical tool. What is the truth about what makes an action or a policy a morally good one, or morally right? But the development of the theory itself was also influenced by strong views about what was wrong in society. The conviction that, for example, some laws are bad resulted in analysis of why they were bad. And, for Jeremy Bentham, what made them bad was their lack of utility, their tendency to lead to unhappiness and misery without any compensating happiness. If a law or an action doesn't do any good, then it isn't any good.

1.3 Jeremy Bentham

Jeremy Bentham (1748–1832) was influenced both by Hobbes' account of human nature and Hume's account of social utility. He famously held that humans were ruled by two sovereign masters – pleasure and pain. We seek pleasure and the avoidance of pain, they "govern us in all we do, in all we say, in all we think".[14] Yet he also promulgated the principle of utility as the standard of right action on the part of governments and individuals. Actions are approved when they are such as to promote happiness, or pleasure, and disapproved of when they have a tendency to cause unhappiness, or pain.[15] Combine this criterion of rightness with a view that we should be actively trying to promote overall happiness, and one has a serious incompatibility with psychological egoism. Thus, his apparent endorsement of Hobbesian psychological egoism created problems in understanding his moral theory since psychological egoism rules out acting to promote the overall well-being when it is incompatible with one's own. For the psychological egoist, that is not even a possibility. So, given 'ought implies can' it would follow that we are not obligated to act to promote overall well-being when that is incompatible with our own. This generates a serious tension in Bentham's thought, one that was drawn to his attention. He sometimes seemed to think that he could reconcile the two commitments empirically, that is, by noting that when people act to promote the good they are helping themselves, too. But this claim only serves to muddy the waters, since the standard understanding of psychological egoism – and Bentham's own statement of his view – identifies motives of action that are self-interested. Yet this seems, again, in conflict with his own specification of the method for making moral decisions, which is not to focus on self-interest – indeed, the addition of extent as a parameter along which to measure pleasure produced distinguishes this approach from ethical egoism. Aware of the difficulty, in later years he seemed to pull back from a full-fledged commitment to psychological egoism, admitting that people do sometimes act benevolently – with the overall good of humanity in mind.

Bentham also benefited from Hume's work, though in many ways their approaches to moral philosophy were completely different. Hume rejected the egoistic view of human nature. Hume also focused on character evaluation in his system. Actions are significant as evidence of character, but have only this derivative significance. In moral evaluation the main concern is that of character. Yet Bentham focused on act evaluation.

There was a tendency in moral philosophy more generally – remarked on by J. B. Schneewind, for example – to move away from focus on character evaluation after Hume and towards act evaluation.[16] Recall that Bentham was enormously interested in social reform. Indeed, reflection on what was morally problematic about laws and policies influenced his thinking on utility as a standard. When one legislates, however, one is legislating in support of, or against, certain actions. Character – that is, a person's true character – is known, if known at all, only by that person. If one finds the opacity of the will thesis plausible then character, while theoretically very interesting, isn't a practical focus for legislation. Further, as Schneewind notes, there was an increasing sense that focus on character would actually be disruptive, socially, particularly if one's view was that a person who didn't agree with one on a moral issues was defective in terms of his or her character, as opposed to simply making a mistake reflected in action.

But Bentham does take from Hume the view that utility is the measure of virtue – that is, utility more broadly construed than in Hume's actual usage of the term. This is because Hume made a distinction between pleasure that the perception of virtue generates in the observer and social utility, which consisted in a trait's having tangible benefits for society, any instance of which may or may not generate pleasure in the observer. But Bentham is not simply reformulating a Humean position – he's merely been influenced by Hume's arguments to see pleasure as a measure or standard of moral value. So, why not move from pleasurable responses to traits to pleasure as a kind of consequence that is good, and in relation to which actions are morally right or wrong? Bentham, in making this move, avoids a problem for Hume. On Hume's view it seems that the response – corrected, to be sure – determines the trait's quality as a virtue or vice. But on Bentham's view the action (or trait) is morally good, right, or virtuous in view of the consequences it generates, the pleasure or utility it produces, which could be completely independent of what our responses are to the trait. So, unless Hume endorses a kind of ideal observer test for virtue, it will be harder for him to account for how it is that people make mistakes in evaluations of virtue and vice. Bentham, on the other hand, can say that people may not respond to the action's good qualities – perhaps they don't perceive the good effects. But as long as there are these good effects that are, on balance, better than the effects of any alternative course of action, then the action is the right one. Rhetorically, anyway, one can see why this is an important move for Bentham to be able to make. He was a social reformer. He felt that people often had responses to certain actions – of pleasure or disgust – that did not reflect anything morally significant at all. Indeed, in his discussions of homosexuality, for example, he explicitly notes that "antipathy" is not sufficient reason to legislate against a practice:

> The circumstances from which this antipathy may have taken its rise may be worth enquiring to. ... One is the physical antipathy to the offence. ... The act is to the highest degree odious and disgusting, that is, not to the man who does it, for he does it only because it gives him pleasure, but to one who thinks [?] of it. Be it so, but what is that to him?[17]

Bentham then notes that people are prone to use their physical antipathy as a pretext to transition to moral antipathy and the attending desire to punish the persons who offend their taste. This is illegitimate on his view for a variety of reasons, one of which is that to punish person for violations of taste, or on the basis of prejudice, would result in runaway punishments, "one should never know where to stop." The prejudice in question can be dealt with by showing it "to be ill-grounded." This reduces the antipathy to the act in question. This demonstrates an optimism in Bentham. If a pain can be demonstrated to be based on false beliefs then he believes that it can be altered or at the very least "assuaged and reduced." This is distinct from the view that a pain or pleasure based on a false belief should be discounted. Bentham does not believe the latter. Thus Bentham's hedonism is a very straightforward hedonism. The one intrinsic good is pleasure, the bad is pain. We are to promote pleasure and act to reduce pain. When called upon to make a moral decision one measures an action's value with respect to pleasure and pain according to the following quantitative parameters: intensity (how strong the pleasure or pain is), duration (how long it lasts), certainty (how likely the pleasure or pain is to be the result of the action), proximity (how close the sensation will be to performance of the action), fecundity (how likely it is to lead to further pleasures or pains), purity (how much intermixture there is with the other sensation). One also considers extent – the number of people affected by the action.

Keeping track of all of these parameters can be complicated and time consuming. Bentham does not recommend that they figure into every act of moral deliberation, because of the efficiency costs that need to be considered. Experience can guide us. We know that the pleasure of kicking someone is generally outweighed by the pain inflicted on that person, so such calculations when confronted with a temptation to kick someone are

unnecessary. It is reasonable to judge it wrong on the basis of past experience or consensus. One can use 'rules of thumb' to guide action, but these
rules are overridable when abiding by them would conflict with the promotion of the good.

Bentham's view was surprising to many at the time, at least in part
because he viewed the moral quality of an action to be determined instrumentally. It isn't so much that there is a particular kind of action that is
intrinsically wrong; actions that are wrong are wrong simply in virtue of
their effects, thus, instrumentally wrong. This cut against the view that there
are some actions that by their very nature are just wrong, regardless of
their effects. Some may be wrong because they are 'unnatural' – and, again,
Bentham would dismiss this as a legitimate criterion. Some may be wrong
because they violate liberty or autonomy. Again, Bentham would view
liberty and autonomy as good – but good instrumentally, not intrinsically.
Thus, any action deemed wrong due to a violation of autonomy is deriva-
tively wrong on instrumental grounds as well. This is interesting in moral
philosophy, as it is far removed from the Kantian approach to moral evaluation as well as from natural law approaches. It is also interesting in terms
of political philosophy and social policy. On Bentham's view the law is not
monolithic and immutable. Since effects of a given policy may change, the
moral quality of the policy may change as well. Nancy Rosenblum noted
that for Bentham one doesn't simply decide on good laws and leave it at
that: "Lawmaking must be recognized as a continual process in response to
diverse and changing desires that require adjustment".[18] A law that is good
at one point in time may be a bad law at some other point in time. Thus,
lawmakers have to be sensitive to changing social circumstances. To be fair
to Bentham's critics, of course, they are free to agree with him that this is
the case in many situations, just not all, and that there is still a subset of laws
that reflect the fact that some actions just are intrinsically wrong regardless
of consequences. Bentham is in the much more difficult position of arguing
that effects are all there is to the moral evaluation of action and policy.

1.4 John Stuart Mill

John Stuart Mill (1806–73) was a follower of Bentham, and, for most of his
life, greatly admired Bentham's work even though he disagreed with some
of Bentham's claims – particularly on the nature of 'happiness'. Bentham,
recall, had held that there were no qualitative differences between pleasures, only quantitative ones. This left him open to a variety of criticisms.

First, Bentham's hedonism was too egalitarian. Simple-minded pleasures, sensual pleasures, were just as good, at least intrinsically, as more sophisticated and complex pleasures. The pleasure of drinking a beer in front of the TV surely doesn't rate as highly as the pleasure one gets solving a complicated math problem, or reading a poem, or listening to Mozart. Second, Bentham's view that there were no qualitative differences in pleasures also left him open to the complaint that on his view human pleasures were of no more value than animal pleasures and, third, committed him to the corollary that the moral status of animals, tied to their sentience, was the same as that of humans. While harming a puppy and harming a person are both bad, most people had the view that harming the person was worse. Mill sought changes to the theory that could accommodate those sorts of intuitions.

To this end, Mill's hedonism was influenced by perfectionist intuitions. There are some pleasures that are more fitting than others. Intellectual pleasures are of a higher, better sort than those that are merely sensual and that we share with animals. To some this seems to mean that Mill really wasn't a hedonistic utilitarian. His view of the good did radically depart from Bentham's view. However, like Bentham, the good still consists in pleasure, it is still a psychological state. There is certainly that similarity. Further, the basic structures of the theories are the same.[19] While it is true that Mill is more comfortable with notions like 'rights' this does not mean that he in fact rejected utilitarianism. The rationale for all the rights he recognizes is utilitarian.

Mill's 'proof' of the claim that intellectual pleasures are better in kind than others, though, is highly suspect. He doesn't attempt a mere appeal to raw intuition. Instead, he argues that those persons who have experienced both view the higher as better than the lower. Who would rather be a happy oyster, living an enormously long life, than a person living a normal life? Or, to use his most famous example, it is better to be Socrates "dissatisfied" than a fool "satisfied." In this way Mill was able to solve a problem for utilitarianism.

Mill also argued that the principle could be proven, using another rather notorious argument:

> The only proof capable of being given that an object is visible is that people actually see it. ... In like manner, I apprehend, the sole evidence it is possible to produce that anything is desirable is that people do actually desire it. If the end which the utilitarian doctrine proposes to itself were

> not, in theory and in practice, acknowledged to be an end, nothing could ever convince any person that it was so.[20]

Mill then continues to argue that people desire happiness – the utilitarian end – and that the general happiness is "a good to the aggregate of all persons" (81).

G. E. Moore (1873–1958) criticized this as fallacious. He argued that it rested on an obvious ambiguity:

> Mill has made as naïve and artless a use of the naturalistic fallacy as anybody could desire. "Good", he tells us, means "desirable", and you can only find out what is desirable by seeking to find out what is actually desired. ... The fact is that "desirable" does not mean "able to be desired" as "visible" means "able to be seen." The desirable means simply what ought to be desired or deserves to be desired; just as the detestable means not what can be but what ought to be detested.[21]

It should be noted, however, that Mill was offering this as an alternative to Bentham's view, which had been itself criticized as a "swine morality," locating the good in pleasure in a kind of indiscriminate way. The distinctions he makes strike many as intuitively plausible ones. Bentham, however, can accommodate many of the same intuitions within his system. This is because, as pointed out above, he notes that there are a variety of parameters along which we quantitatively measure pleasure – intensity and duration are just two of those. His complete list is the following: intensity, duration, certainty or uncertainty, propinquity or remoteness, fecundity, purity, and extent. Thus, what Mill calls the intellectual pleasures will score more highly than the sensual ones along several parameters, and this could give us reason to prefer those pleasures – but it is a quantitative not a qualitative reason, on Bentham's view. When a student decides to study for an exam rather than go to a party, for example, she is making the best decision even though she is sacrificing short-term pleasure. That's because studying for the exam, Bentham could argue, scores higher in terms of the long-term pleasures doing well in school leads to, as well as the fecundity of the pleasure in leading to yet other pleasures. However, Bentham will have to concede that the very happy oyster that lives a very long time could, in principle, have a better life than a normal human.

Mill's version of utilitarianism differed from Bentham's also in that he placed weight on the effectiveness of internal sanctions – emotions like guilt and remorse that serve to regulate our actions. This is an offshoot of the different view of human nature adopted by Mill. We are the sorts of beings that have social feelings, feelings for others, not just ourselves. We care about them, and when we perceive harms to them this causes painful experiences in us. When one perceives oneself to be the agent of that harm, the negative emotions are centered on the self. One feels guilt for what one has done, not for what one sees another doing. Like external forms of punishment, internal sanctions are instrumentally very important to appropriate action. Mill also held that natural features of human psychology, such as conscience and a sense of justice, underwrite motivation. The sense of justice, for example, results from very natural impulses. Part of this sense involves a desire to punish those who have harmed others, and this desire in turn "is a spontaneous outgrowth from two sentiments, both in the highest degree natural … the impulse of self-defense, and the feeling of sympathy."[22] Of course, he goes on, the justification must be a separate issue. The feeling is there naturally, but it is our "enlarged" sense, our capacity to include the welfare of others in our considerations and to make intelligent decisions, that gives it the right normative force.

Like Bentham, Mill sought to use utilitarianism to inform law and social policy. The aim of increasing happiness underlies his arguments for women's suffrage and free speech. We can be said to have certain rights, then, but those rights are underwritten by utility. If one can show that a purported right or duty is harmful, then one has shown that it is not genuine. One of Mill's most famous arguments to this effect can be found in his writing on women's suffrage when he discusses the ideal marriage of partners, noting that the ideal exists between individuals of "cultivated faculties" who influence each other equally. Improving the social status of women was important because they were capable of these cultivated faculties, and denying them access to education and other opportunities for development is forgoing a significant source of happiness. Further, the men who would deny women the opportunity for education, self-improvement, and political expression do so out of base motives, and the resulting pleasures are not ones that are of the best sort.

Bentham and Mill both attacked social traditions that were justified by appeals to natural order. The correct appeal is to utility itself. Traditions often turned out to be "relics" of "barbarous" times, and appeals to nature as a form of justification were just ways to try to rationalize continued deference to those relics.

1.5 Henry Sidgwick

Henry Sidgwick's (1838–1900) *The Methods of Ethics* (1874) is one of the best-known works in utilitarian moral philosophy, and deservedly so. It offers a defense of utilitarianism, though some writers have argued that it should not primarily be read as a defense of utilitarianism.[23] In *Methods* Sidgwick is concerned with developing an account of "the different methods of Ethics that I find implicit in our common moral reasoning." These methods are egoism, intuition-based morality, and utilitarianism. On Sidgwick's view, utilitarianism is the more basic theory. A simple reliance on intuition, for example, cannot resolve fundamental conflicts between values, or rules, such as truth and justice that may conflict. In Sidgwick's words, "we require some higher principle to decide the issue." That will be utilitarianism. Further, the rules which seem to be a fundamental part of common-sense morality are often vague and underdescribed, and applying them will actually require appeal to something theoretically more basic – again, utilitarianism. Yet further, absolute interpretations of rules seem highly counterintuitive, and yet we need some justification for any exceptions – provided, again, by utilitarianism. Sidgwick provides a compelling case for the theoretical primacy of utilitarianism.

Sidgwick was also a British philosopher, and his views developed out of and in response to those of Bentham and Mill. His *Methods* offer an engagement with the theory as it had been presented before him, and was an exploration of it and the main alternatives as well as a defense.

Sidgwick was also concerned with clarifying fundamental features of the theory, and in this respect his account has been enormously influential to later writers, not only to utilitarians and consequentialists, generally, but to intuitionists as well. Sidgwick's thorough and penetrating discussion of the theory raised many of the concerns that have been developed by recent moral philosophers.

One extremely controversial feature of Sidgwick's views relates to his rejection of a publicity requirement for moral theory. He writes:

> Thus, the Utilitarian conclusion, carefully stated, would seem to be this; that the opinion that secrecy may render an action right which would not otherwise be so should itself be kept comparatively secret; and similarly it seems expedient that the doctrine that esoteric morality is expedient should itself be kept esoteric. Or, if this concealment be difficult to maintain, it may be desirable that Common Sense should repudiate the

doctrines which it is expedient to confine to an enlightened few. And thus a Utilitarian may reasonably desire, on Utilitarian principles, that some of his conclusions should be rejected by mankind generally; or even that the vulgar should keep aloof from his system as a whole, in so far as the inevitable indefiniteness and complexity of its calculations render it likely to lead to bad results in their hands.[24]

This accepts that utilitarianism may be self-effacing; that is, that it may be best if people do not believe it, even though it is true. Further, it rendered the theory subject to Bernard Williams' criticism that the theory really simply reflected the colonial elitism of Sidgwick's time, that it was 'Government House utilitarianism'. The elitism in his remarks may reflect a broader attitude, one in which the educated are considered better policy-makers than the uneducated.[25]

One issue raised in the above remarks is relevant to practical deliberation in general. To what extent should proponents of a given theory, or a given rule, or a given policy – or even proponents of a given one-off action – consider what they think people will actually do, as opposed to what they think those same people ought to do (under full and reasonable reflection, for example)? This is an example of something that comes up in the actualism–possibilism debate in accounts of practical deliberation. Extrapolating from the example used above, we have people who advocate telling the truth, or what they believe to be the truth, even if the effects are bad as a result of the truth being misused by others. On the other hand are those who recommend not telling the truth when it is predicted that the truth will be misused by others to achieve bad results. Of course it is the case that the truth ought not be misused, that its misuse can be avoided and is not inevitable, but the misuse is entirely predictable. Sidgwick seems to be recommending that we follow the course that we predict will have the best outcome, given as part of our calculations the data that others may fail in some way – either due to having bad desires, or simply not being able to reason effectively. The worry Williams points to really isn't a worry specifically with utilitarianism. Sidgwick would point out that if it is bad to hide the truth, because 'Government House' types, for example, typically engage in self-deceptive rationalizations of their policies (which seems entirely plausible), then one shouldn't do it. And, of course, that heavily influences our intuitions.

Sidgwick raised issues that run much deeper to our basic understanding of utilitarianism. For example, the way earlier utilitarians characterized the principle of utility left open serious indeterminacies. The major one rests on the distinction between total and average utility. He raised the issue in the context of population growth and increasing utility levels by increasing numbers of people (or sentient beings):

> Assuming, then, that the average happiness of human beings is a positive quantity, it seems clear that, supposing the average happiness enjoyed remains undiminished, Utilitarianism directs us to make the number enjoying it as great as possible. But if we foresee as possible that an increase in numbers will be accompanied by a decrease in average happiness or vice versa, a point arises which has not only never been formally noticed, but which seems to have been substantially overlooked by many Utilitarians. For if we take Utilitarianism to prescribe, as the ultimate end of action, happiness on the whole, and not any individual's happiness, unless considered as an element of the whole, it would follow that, if the additional population enjoy on the whole positive happiness, we ought to weigh the amount of happiness gained by the extra number against the amount lost by the remainder.[26]

For Sidgwick, the conclusion on this issue is not to simply strive to greater average utility, but to increase population to the point where we maximize the product of the number of persons who are currently alive and the amount of average happiness. So it seems to be a hybrid, total–average view. This discussion also raised the issue of policy with respect to population growth, and both would be pursued in more detail by later writers, most notably Derek Parfit.[27]

1.6 Ideal utilitarianism

G. E. Moore strongly disagreed with the hedonistic value theory adopted by the classical utilitarians. Moore agreed that we ought to promote the good, but believed that the good included far more than what could be reduced to pleasure. He was a pluralist, rather than a monist, regarding intrinsic value. For example, he believed that 'beauty' was an intrinsic good. A beautiful object had value independent of any pleasure it might generate in a viewer. Moore thus differed from Sidgwick, who regarded the good as consisting in some consciousness. Some objective states in the world are intrinsically good, and on Moore's view, beauty is just such a state. He used one of his more notorious thought experiments to make this point: he asked the reader to compare two worlds: one was entirely beautiful, full of things which complemented each other; the other was a hideous, ugly world, filled with "everything that is most disgusting to us." Further, there are no human beings, one must imagine, around to appreciate or be disgusted by the worlds. The question then is, which of these worlds is better, which one's existence would be better than the other's? Of course, Moore believed it was clear that the beautiful world was better, even though no one was around to appreciate its beauty. This emphasis on beauty was one facet of Moore's work that made him a darling of the Bloomsbury Group. If beauty was a part of the good independent of its effects on the psychological states of others – independent, really, of how it affected others – then one needn't sacrifice morality on the altar of beauty anymore. Following beauty is not a mere indulgence, but may even be a moral obligation. Though Moore himself certainly never applied his view to such cases, it does provide the resources for dealing with what the contemporary literature has dubbed 'admirable immorality' cases, at least some of them. Gauguin may have abandoned his wife and children, but it was to a beautiful end.

Moore's targets in arguing against hedonism were the earlier utilitarians, who argued that the good was some state of consciousness such as pleasure. He actually waffled on this issue a bit, but always disagreed with hedonism in that even when he held that beauty all by itself was not an intrinsic good, he also held that for the appreciation of beauty to be a good the beauty must actually be there, in the world, and not be the result of illusion.

Moore further criticized the view that pleasure itself was an intrinsic good, since it failed a kind of isolation test that he proposed for intrinsic value. If one compared an empty universe with a universe of sadists occupied with cruel thoughts, the empty universe would strike one as better. This is true even though there is a good deal of pleasure, and no pain (as stipulated) in the universe of sadists. This would seem to indicate that what is necessary for the good is at least the absence of bad intentionality. The pleasures of sadists, in virtue of their desires to harm others, get discounted – they are not good, even though they are pleasures. Note this radical departure from Bentham, who held that even malicious pleasure was intrinsically good, and, if no instrumental bad attached to the pleasure, it was wholly good as well.

One of Moore's important contributions was to put forward an 'organic unity' or 'organic whole' view of value. The principle of organic unity is vague, and there is some disagreement about what Moore actually meant in presenting it. Moore states that 'organic' is used "to denote the fact that a whole has an intrinsic value different in amount from the sum of the values of its parts."[28] And, for Moore, that is all it is supposed to denote. So, for example, one cannot determine the value of a body by adding up the value of its parts. Some parts of the body may have value only in relation to the whole. An arm or a leg, for example, may have no value at all separated from the body, but have a great deal of value when attached to the body, and even increase the value of the body. In the section of *Principia Ethica* on the Ideal, the principle of organic unity comes into play in noting that when persons experience pleasure through perception of something beautiful (which involves a positive emotion in the face of a recognition of an appropriate object – an emotive and cognitive set of elements), the experience of the beauty is better when the object of the experience, the beautiful object, actually exists. The idea was that experiencing beauty has a small positive value, and existence of beauty has a small positive value, but combining them has a great deal of value, more than the simple addition of the two small values.[29] Moore noted: "A true belief in the reality of an object greatly increases the value of many valuable wholes."[30]

This principle in Moore – particularly as applied to the significance of actual existence and value, or knowledge and value – provided utilitarians with tools to meet some significant challenges. For example, deluded happiness would be severely lacking on Moore's view, especially in comparison to happiness based on knowledge.

Since the early twentieth century utilitarianism has undergone a variety of refinements. Since the middle of the twentieth century it has become more common to identify it as a 'consequentialist' approach since very few philosophers agree entirely with the view proposed by the classical utilitarians, particularly with respect to the hedonistic value theory. But the influence of the classical utilitarians has been profound – not only within moral philosophy, but within political philosophy and social policy. The question Bentham asked – "What use is it?" – is a cornerstone of policy formation. It is a completely secular, forward-looking question. The articulation and systematic development of this approach to policy formation are owed to the classical utilitarians. In the remainder of this book we will examine how utilitarianism changed in light of criticisms to the more general 'consequentialism'. The core insight remained the same, however, in a deep commitment to consequences in determining the moral quality of actions and character.

Chapter summary

This chapter provides an overview of the history of consequentialism as an approach to moral evaluation, focusing on utilitarianism, the most prominent form of consequentialism. Utilitarianism holds that the right action is the one that produces the greatest good for the greatest number of people. Further, for the classical utilitarians, Jeremy Bentham and John Stuart Mill, the most fundamental good was pleasure (absence of pain). Bentham and Mill disagreed over the nature of pleasure, and later writers, also discussed in the chapter, challenged their hedonistic theory of value. Moore, for example, believed that there were intrinsic goods other than pleasure, such as beauty.

Further reading

For classical utilitarianism and contemporary criticism and discussion, see: John Stuart Mill, *Utilitarianism*, ed. Roger Crisp (New York: Oxford University Press, 1998); Jeremy Bentham, *The Principles of Morals and Legislation*; Henry Sidgwick, *The Methods of Ethics* (Indianapolis, IN: Hackett Publishing Co., 1981); G. E. Moore, *Principia Ethica* (Amherst, NY: Prometheus Books, 1988).

For a general historical overview, see Geoffrey Scarre, *Utilitarianism* (London: Routledge, 1996).

2

VALUE AND MAXIMIZATION

1.1 Value: greatest *happiness*

As noted in the first chapter, consequentialist theories of moral evaluation have two parts – the part that specifies what is of *intrinsic value*, and the part that specifies how value is to be approached, promoted, or aggregated. In this chapter we first discuss value and the different ways in which consequentialist theories have specified intrinsic value. We then discuss aggregation.

One of the central tenets of consequentialism has been a commitment to *neutral* value. Neutral value is value specified without reference to a particular individual. If pleasure has value, on this approach, it doesn't matter *whose* pleasure it is. Neutral value is understood in contrast to *relative* value. A value is relative if it does make reference to particular persons. If one regards one's friend's pleasure as more valuable than that of a stranger, then one is committed to relative value. That the pleasure is your friend's makes it something special. Until recently, consequentialists denied relative value. For now we will consider the different approaches to value as neutral. Everyone's good counts the same. This has been thought to lead to problems for consequentialism, since it seems to run counter to the view that we *ought* to give special consideration to the good of those near and dear to us. We will take up this problem later in the book.

One way to approach the issue is to ask: what is it that makes our lives, fundamentally, go well? What is good for a person? Imagine making a list of all the things that one thinks of as 'good' – things that make one's life go well. One's list might include all kinds of things that have nothing to do with morality *per se*, things like 'friendship', 'music', 'art', 'artisanal cheeses', 'my pet dog', and so on. We think of these things as 'goods', and one person's list can differ quite dramatically from another person's. Sally might love cheese, and Bob hate it. Now, no plausible value theory would list 'cheese' as an *intrinsic* good. It is not good *in and of itself*. Rather, cheese, if it is good, is good *instrumentally*. It is good, as far as Sally is concerned, because of its effects – as is the case for 'TV' or 'shag carpeting' and so on. What is it that makes cheese good, if it is good? A reasonable first response would be something like 'happiness'. Sally thinks of cheese as good because she enjoys it. The taste of cheese contributes to her happiness. This is not, of course, a full response. The burden then shifts to providing an account of happiness as an intrinsic good, and then defending it against counterexamples.

Recall from Chapter 1 that the classical utilitarians, Bentham and Mill, offered a hedonistic account of well-being, or happiness. That is, they viewed the basic good for a person as consisting in pleasure and/or the avoidance of pain. Though they agree on this, there is much disagreement between them on how to unpack the details. It is clear that for Bentham we understand pleasure purely subjectively, as a kind of feeling that attends certain experiences. Though there are different parameters along which we can measure pleasures, for Bentham they are essentially of the same kind. No pleasure by its very nature is superior in kind to another pleasure. Pleasures vary only in terms of quantity, not quality. Mill famously disagreed with this view of pleasure, arguing that there were indeed qualitative distinctions to be made between the 'higher' and 'lower' pleasures. The higher pleasures involve our cognitive capacities in ways the lower pleasures do not. A human being who experiences higher-level pleasures, as well as certain pains, has a better life than an oyster that feels low-level pleasure burrowed in the warm mud. The oyster is simply incapable of experiencing the best sort of pleasure. Its life is not as good as that of the person.

Many commentators on Mill believed that this account showed Mill to be rejecting hedonism, since he seemed to be rejecting a *purely* subjective standard of value. On Mill's view the pleasure one gets from reading a good poem is better than the pleasure one gets from eating an ice cream cone, even if the latter is quantitatively superior (i.e. superior in terms of intensity, duration, etc.). Further, the pleasure one gets from reading a good poem is better even if the agent does not herself think it is. Thus, the standard is not purely subjective. But this is going beyond what Mill actually said. His view is a kind of hedonism, but modified to give priority to some pleasures over others.

Even modified hedonism of the sort espoused by Mill has problems that are really endemic to subjective accounts. G. E. Moore argued that a good test for intrinsic value is an *isolation test*: basically, if something is good in isolation, considered completely independent of consequences, then it is intrinsically good. Pleasure does not pass this test, because one can imagine pleasure, considered in isolation, which is *not* good. The pleasure of a sadist, for example, is not good even when that pleasure does not and cannot lead to bad effects. J. J. C. Smart took Moore's discussion of this as a starting point in defending hedonism. Smart asks us to consider two universes. One is empty. One contains only a sadist who is deluded – who believes that he is in fact harming others, and who is deriving enormous pleasure from the harm he believes he is inflicting. Moore's view is that the empty universe is better than the universe containing the deluded sadist, even though the sadist is not actually harming anyone. Smart argued that, contrary to what Moore believed about sadistic pleasure, "the universe containing the deluded sadist is the preferable one. After all, he is happy, and since there is no other sentient being, what harm can he do?"[1] Of course, this is unpalatable, but one reason might be that our intuitions about these cases are formed under normal circumstances, which certainly don't apply in the thought experiment. Normally, sadistic people cause all kinds of harm.

There are other tests for intrinsic value besides the isolation test. For example, the *constancy test*, which is often confused with the isolation test. The constancy test holds that something is intrinsically good if it is good in *any possible context*. Here one is not extrapolating *away* from effects, but instead varying one's consideration of the putative intrinsic good from context to context, from one set of effects to another. This test often takes the form: would x (the putative good) still be good *even* if it gave rise to bad effects? Take pleasure again – there does seem to be something good about pleasure itself, even in those situations where the pleasure might lead one astray. Perhaps I decide to eat the extra portion of chocolate cake. I derive a good deal of pleasure from this, though of course, down the road, it will hurt me. But the pleasure in *itself* is good, though instrumentally, in this particular case, it is bad. Compare this to some object, like my shampoo. Whatever is good about my shampoo can be understood only in terms of its effects. If I ask, "would my shampoo be good even if it didn't clean my hair?" the answer would be "no." In this case, varying the effects reveals that shampoo is only instrumentally good, and is not intrinsically good.

Another test, and one that I used to introduce hedonism, is that of *conceptual primacy*: in virtue of what is something good? The basic, or intrinsic, good comes at the end of the explanatory, or conceptual, chain. Pleasure does well on this test, since it is difficult to imagine anything further back which would account for pleasure's goodness. Pleasure has the advantage of providing an intuitively plausible common ground for our value judgments.

These tests can be combined. Moore, for example, argued that pleasure was not the only intrinsic good, at least, by noting that we can imagine two worlds – one beautiful, the other hideous – in which there are no sentient beings, and still judge the beautiful better than the hideous, even though neither contained pleasure or pain. So, if that observation holds, beauty is still good in isolation, and its goodness cannot be completely accounted for by reduction to pleasure.

The classical utilitarians didn't distinguish these tests for intrinsic value, but it is likely that they would have thought pleasure to have passed these tests. The major difficulty would be holding that pleasure is the *only* thing that in fact passes these tests. Some critics of hedonism tend to argue that even though pleasure is good for a person, it is not the only intrinsic good – this was one of Moore's maneuvers when it came to understanding the good. Others tend to argue that the strong intuitions that favor pleasure are confused – that it is other subjective features of a person which correlate with pleasure that really account for a person's good. We will consider these options later.

Another famous problem for hedonism, raised by Robert Nozick, is that of the experience machine. Suppose that Anthony has been kidnapped by a mad scientist who hooks him up to a machine that will feed pleasurable experiences into his brain. Anthony does not know he is in a laboratory, having experiences fed into his brain. Instead, he believes he is in Paris, at the Louvre, enjoying art. On the hedonist's view this state of affairs is just as good as the state of affairs in which Anthony really is in Paris enjoying a tour of the Louvre. But this seems strongly counterintuitive – it isn't just pleasure that matters, but we also think that the pleasure has to be caused the right way – caused by events reflected in the experiences themselves, not by completely unrelated events. Some philosophers argue that the pleasures need to be 'veridical' in this way – they need to reflect reality. This is widely viewed as a compelling counterexample to hedonism.

Can hedonism be resurrected? One way might be to introduce some objective constraint on pleasures that are to count. This would certainly run against the Bentham brand of hedonism, but would be in keeping with

Mill's views. Mill seemed to have the view that some pleasures would just not be fitting for a human being to experience. One plausible example would be experiencing pleasure in an innocent person's pain. What exactly makes this pleasure 'unfitting', 'false', or 'inappropriate' is an interesting, though separate, issue. One might hold, for example, a hybrid of hedonism and perfectionism, and maintain that human excellences are tied up with our natural capacity to engage sympathetically with others, and that pleasure in the pain of an innocent person falls short of this sympathetic engagement. One might also take an approach that ties the moral with the epistemic. Perhaps pleasures are 'false' if based on false beliefs, including false normative beliefs. The person who takes pleasure in the pain of an innocent person implicitly endorses that pain as good − which is false: that pain is actually a bad thing, in and of itself, on the hedonistic view. Note that with this strategy we can explain why we place such significance on true belief. The problem with this approach to helping the hedonist, however, is that it seems to go too far. There are times when false pleasures seem morally or prudentially good, even if they are epistemically defective. These will be cases where living an illusion is the best option for a person. If one's life in the real world would be nasty, brutish, and short, then maybe life in the Matrix isn't bad − except in the epistemic sense of relying on false belief. One could nevertheless hold that in general false beliefs do seem to undermine our level of happiness, so that there is at least *pro tanto* reason to avoid them, and not endorse them, though there will be situations in which false beliefs turn out to have positive effects for the agent. There are a variety of ways this avenue of thought could be developed.

Another attempt at shoring up hedonism is presented in Fred Feldman's account of hedonism in terms of *propositional pleasure*.[2] On this view when a person experiences pleasure he 'takes pleasure in x' or 'is pleased about x'. However, pleasure on this view is not a sensory feeling. Feldman uses the example of someone who has been anesthetized and yet is still pleased that the war in Bosnia has ended. He can be pleased about this intrinsically or extrinsically − that is, for its own sake or for the sake of something else. Thus, pleasure in the sense of intrinsically valuable experience is not the raw, subjective, positive feeling. It involves, instead, having a positive attitude towards something that can be expressed in a proposition.

This approach has the advantage of dealing with an objection that Sidgwick raised against hedonism: that there is no single, unified, phenomenology of pleasure. Pleasures all have a different tone to them − so the pleasure one gets from eating ice cream is very different from the pleasure one gets from reading a great novel, which in turn is also different from the pleasure one gets in chatting with a friend. On this view one has a pleasure feeling state, but what makes it pleasure is the attitude, the pro-attitude, one has towards it.

In a way Feldman seems to go too far. One of the great advantages of the approach championed by both Bentham and Mill was that it was able to hold that the positive experiences of animals had intrinsic value. Yet animals are not capable of having attitudes with respect to *propositions*. Propositions are the objects of belief states, the things that are considered true or false; when Mary believes that snow is white, 'snow is white' is the propositional content of her belief. Animals don't seem to have psychological states with propositional content. They lack the necessary linguistic abilities. Feldman's view of value loses that advantage. However, there are ways of under-standing locutions such as "Fido takes pleasure in chewing on my shoe" which don't require that Fido have an attitude towards a proposition. For example, one could say that Fido's pleasure is taken not in a proposition but in a *state of affairs*, the state of affairs involving my shoe getting chewed by him. States of affairs are not linguistic entities at all, they are not the sorts of things that have truth value. Further, one might hold that we need an account of pleasure as valuable that is mixed – similar to the sort of view that Mill proposed. Mill was not denying that lower pleasures had value – of course they did. He simply held that the higher pleasures were superior to the lower, so that if one were to choose one would choose a life that had the higher as opposed to one devoid of the higher. Further, there is nothing in the concept of 'intrinsic' that would preclude viewing both pleasures as intrinsically good. Thus, one could argue that there are sensory pleas-ures that are intrinsically good (and we can argue about whether there is some common element to these pleasures, but like Feldman I am inclined to doubt this), and there are pleasures that involve some sort of cognitive or rational element and these, also, are intrinsically good, and perhaps even better than the first.

Another problem is that on this account either the attitude theorist holds that all that matters is the pro-attitude itself – that is, approving of the emotional response – or that it also matters that there is a positive hedonic tone as well. The first is implausible, for reasons outlined by Timothy Sprigge.[3] There are all kinds of feelings we approve of, which we wouldn't want to call 'pleasure'. A guilt-ridden person might approve of the pain he feels as he is punished for his crime, but it would be odd to refer to this as pleasure, and precisely because it seems to lack the requisite hedonic tone.

But if we opt for the second construal, and claim that there also has to be a positive hedonic tone, the attitude theorist isn't able to bypass the issue that there just doesn't seem to be a common hedonic tone to these experiences.

The other side of the hedonistic equation is that pain is the one *intrinsic* bad. Keep in mind this doesn't mean that it is never good – just that when it's good it is only good instrumentally, as a means to some other end. Like the positive side of the equation, this claim has been roundly attacked as failing to account for harms that a person is not aware of, and that don't involve a feeling of pain. Technically, of course, in a bad situation the good may involve reducing pain rather than generating a positive state, or an *absolutely* positive state. This is important, because in a given context the rational thing is to select among one's alternatives according to the best hedonic tone available amongst the range of options. To pick a rather horrible example, suppose that Bill's foot is trapped in a bear trap and his choice is between dying from shock and dehydration, because he won't be able to escape with the trap on his leg, or cutting his own foot off, which would be painful. Both options are very bad, and the choice isn't between doing something pleasurable versus doing something painful. The choice is between two bad options, two painful options, and selecting the least painful of the two.

1.2 'Higher' pleasures

There were two parts to Mill's argument that there is a qualitative, and not just quantitative, distinction to be made between pleasures. The first part had to do with making the distinction between higher and lower pleasures. The second part had to do with providing an argument that the higher are superior in kind to the lower.

In making the distinction Mill observes that there must be some distinction between kinds of pleasures to account for the difference between human happiness and swine happiness: "Human beings have faculties more elevated than the animal appetites, and when once made conscious of them, do not regard anything as happiness which does not include their gratification".[4] For pigs, then, there are the "pleasures of mere sensation" but for human beings there is more – there are also the "pleasures of the intellect, of the feelings and imagination, and of the moral sentiments".[5]

But the argument rests not simply on making a distinction, but also on noting that the pleasures of the intellect are superior to mere sensory pleasures. It is of course possible to argue the other way – that there are these two kinds of pleasures, and the sensory ones are superior in value; it is also possible to hold that there are these two kinds of pleasures, yet one is not superior in kind to the other. Of course, in the latter case, there would be little point to producing the distinction in discussing the merits of hedonism.

How does Mill argue for the superiority of the intellectual pleasures? Here we get the argument that, amongst those who have experienced both sorts of pleasure, the opinion that the intellectual ones are better in kind is universal. We would, for the most part, prefer to be "Socrates dissatisfied" rather than a "fool, satisfied." Those who disagree are anomalies who are lacking in judgment.

Again, some read into Mill at this point a *rejection* of hedonism. They argue that this argument shows Mill to be a kind of perfectionist – someone who values things like accomplishment over sensory pleasure. But Mill is simply arguing for a different kind of hedonism, one that holds that pleasures vary in kind, yet good is still understood completely in terms of these pleasures. His theory of value might be termed a form of *hedonistic pluralism*, since there are two kinds of pleasure both of which have intrinsic value. The value of intellectual pleasures is not reducible to the sensory; neither is the value of sensory pleasure reducible to the intellectual.

Let's look at each part of Mill's argument. First, the distinction itself. How might we understand more fully the distinction between higher and lower pleasures? A case of the former would be something like the pleasure one gets in reading a poem; a case of the latter would be the pleasure one feels in taking a mud bath.

Intellectual pleasures can be based upon beliefs – indeed, they must be based upon beliefs that one has. Sensory pleasures need not be, though they may be. Though pleasures, strictly speaking, may not be true or false, they may be based upon true or false beliefs, and thus we can loosely speak of true and false pleasures. Imagine that one is watching a play in which there is a truly stunning death scene. The acting seems superb! Then one finds out that the actor has in fact died, that he was not acting in that scene, that it was real. One's initial pleasure in the scene was based on a false belief that he was acting. The pleasure will dissolve once one finds out that the belief it was based upon was false.[6]

In the case of intellectual pleasures, then, we have an underlying issue of normativity – those based on true beliefs will be better than those based on false beliefs. This is a discounting thesis only; it does not imply that those based on false beliefs are worthless. They may be, they may not. There would have to be some other consideration or argument, however, to settle this question. The claim at hand at this point is merely that those based on false beliefs are, *ceteris paribus*, less valuable than those based on true beliefs. Note that it does not follow from this claim that there is no fool's paradise. Even if it is true that pleasure in x is better when x actually obtains than when it does not, a person may not have that option. It may be that the only relevant option would involve pain. It may also be that a non-veridical pleasure in y is better than a veridical pleasure in x, as in the Matrix case mentioned earlier.

Though hedonism in one form or another has enjoyed a slight revival in recent years, most philosophers reject it in favor of some other theory of value.[7] Those who still opt for a subjective theory will hold that the good is understood in terms of preference or desire satisfaction; those who opt for a mixed or objective view hold that good also includes things like 'achievement' which may or may not generate pleasure, but are still good nonetheless.

1.3 Preferences and desires

Attempts to avoid some of the problems with hedonism but still retain a subjective account of value are captured in approaches that tie human good to preference or desire satisfaction. Thus, one could argue that what is good for a person is that her preferences be satisfied. Given a person has a preference for veridicality of her experiences, then Matrix-style scenarios are bad for her even if she gets pleasure while embedded in the Matrix. So these views can avoid the 'experience machine' problem. Preferences and desires are both states that have a 'world to mind' direction of fit. A person satisfies her desires by bringing the world into conformity with the content of the desire.

Technically, of course, preferences and desires are distinct. '*A* prefers p over q' expresses that in a two-choice situation between p and q, A is disposed to choose p. When we speak of someone's preferences, we are talking about how they rank various alternatives. Roughly, '*A* desires p' expresses the fact that A has a mental state such that, all other things being equal, A is disposed to bring about a state of affairs in which p obtains. One can know a lot about a person's preferences, or their ranking of options, without knowing much about what they really want in a given situation.[8] Thus, one may prefer p to q, but not desire p at all. But in the sense that preference satisfaction and desire satisfaction are theories of value, they will be roughly the same. To say Alice has a preference for p over q means that she desires p relative to q.

Thus, though preferences and desires are themselves distinct, preference and desire satisfaction views of value suffer from the same basic sorts of problems and will be discussed together here.

In addition to providing a way to avoid the 'experience machine' problem, these views also have the advantage over hedonism in accounting for what is bad about being dead. Of course, on the hedonist view death is not good, but since there is no pain when one is dead, it also seems to follow from hedonism that death is not bad. This is highly counterintuitive. But preference satisfaction theorists can hold that when someone dies a set of her preferences goes unfulfilled, and that is what makes death bad for her.

However, this type of subjective state theory doesn't avoid all of the problems of hedonism – it has its own version of the sadistic pleasure problem, since an agent could have sadistic pleasures whose satisfaction, on this view, would be good for the agent. Of course, the preference satisfaction theorist can just accept this, holding that we think of these persons as morally bad because they harm others, but that their preferences – even evil ones – are satisfied is still a good for them. Thus, they could draw a distinction between something being good for the agent as opposed to others, and note that when we call something 'good' there is implicit praise involved, which would not all be actually implied by this view.

But another problem is that the very open-endedness of preferences, which seemed to serve a function in accounting for the badness of death, generates other problems. Derek Parfit noted, for example, that sometimes people have preferences that, intuitively, seem very disconnected from their well-being.[9] Suppose that someone has a desire or a preference to be remembered 5,000 years into the future. Has that person's life gone badly if, in fact, she is not remembered 5,000 years into the future? Parfit notes that on the success theory of well-being, this would constitute a harm only if the preference were crucial to the way she actually lived her life. So, if one of her life projects centered on being remembered in the distant future, then she was harmed.[10] This seems quite plausible. We can term this kind of preference *operational* for her, since it shaped her life projects – perhaps she made sure to build monuments with her name on them that would withstand erosion for at least 5,000 years, for example. An operational preference or desire would be contrasted with a *passive* one – one that doesn't guide the agent's life projects. Failure of satisfaction of these preferences does not harm the person, that is, does not in and of itself cause the person's life to have gone less well than otherwise.

But preference satisfaction, like hedonism, is a subjective account of value. Both accounts are criticized for the inability to count as goods things which have no connection to the agent's psychology – things which are good or bad on the basis, it is argued, of objective rather than subjective considerations.

1.4 Objective list theories

The problem with subjective accounts is that they are … subjective. We can always seem to come up with cases that push us to the conclusion that reality matters to value, not simply perceived, or apparent, reality and not just certain subjective states that may or may not reflect appreciation of objective value.

The biggest question for this theory is, what should go on this list? And it should be answered in a way that is not ad hoc. The way this is generally approached is through a canvassing of our intuitions about cases, given some of the tests for value discussed earlier in this chapter. As our discussion of Mill's views made clear, we do seem to have this strong perfectionist streak in our intuitions about value. The pleasure someone gets from counting blades of grass just doesn't seem as good as the pleasure someone gets from solving a difficult math problem, climbing a mountain, or finishing a paper. This speaks to the intuition that genuine achievement or accomplishment is important to us. Further, though this is not Mill's view, it may even be important to us independently of any pleasure considerations.

One philosopher who has recently developed this line of thought is Thomas Hurka.[11] Hurka maintains a view that is similar to the Aristotelian view. Human beings have a certain nature, and certain natural capacities and abilities. Our good consists, basically, in perfecting those. Thus, knowledge counts as an intrinsic good regardless of any pleasure it leads to, because acquiring knowledge involves perfecting our rational capacities. What this means in specific cases is that it may be good for Michael, for example, that he go to graduate school and develop his talent for classical languages – he really is very, very good at classical languages and would contribute a great deal to the field – even though Michael doesn't really want to. He would much rather take up lounging on a beach reading mystery novels. It's not that it would be good for the world that Michael go to grad school – the claim here is that it would be good for *him* to do that. His life is better for the accomplishment, even if he would go to sleep every night dreaming of beaches and Miss Marple.

Some complaints about this approach mirror the disagreement between Bentham and Mill in the arena of hedonism. Bentham's view appears more egalitarian since, if you enjoy spending your time lounging on the beach, and nothing else would give you more pleasure, that is good for you. Mill seems more elitist in that he is putting more significance on intellectual pursuits. For a perfectionist, of course, a lot rests on what is to be perfected, but most put a great weight on intellectual pursuits. This is because reason, intelligence, our cognitive capacities are the ones that distinguish us from other beings in what we regard to be a positive way. These capacities seem to underlie our views that our lives are better than the lives of animals. As such, it is these that perfectionism tends to focus on.

An objective list theorist, then, who takes perfectionism seriously, will hold that pleasure is good but not the only intrinsic good. There is also intrinsic value to developing our rational capacities, pushing ourselves to achieve, and so forth. Martha Nussbaum develops an account of well-being that includes, on the list, practical deliberation.[12] On her view, part of a person's good is being able to *reflect* about what is good for her and make plans. This is a good irrespective of its instrumental benefits. This is because reflection *constitutes* part of what it is to be good as a human being. This is the sort of consideration that Mill was trying to capture in distinguishing the higher from the lower pleasures. There's something superior in kind about the higher pleasures since they involve use of rational capacities.

Thus, hedonists could agree with the view that reflection is very good indeed, but argue that the goods of reflection are compatible with hedonism: Mill, by holding that reflective pleasures are the best sort, and Bentham, by holding that reflection is instrumentally *very* important. While, in principle, push-pin may be as good as poetry, simply in terms of its intrinsic value, the pleasures of reflection are more 'fecund' – they lead to greater pleasures in the future, since our capacity to reason enables us to better achieve our aims, and achieving our aims is correlated with happiness.

Of course, there are many other candidates for intrinsic goods to add to the objective list, goods that are thought to be a component in the best human life: friendship, autonomy, love, for example. Inasmuch as one believes the good of none of these can be reduced to pleasure, these are other candidates for the list. Lately, in the literature critical of consequentialism, for example, a good many people have argued that friendship is a real problem for the classical consequentialist. It looks as if the theorist who does not regard friendship as an intrinsic good is committed to holding it only instrumentally good, and this seems quite incompatible with the nature of friendship itself.

The worry about this general approach is that – aside from theoretical difficulties – one loses prescriptive force. Apparent counterexamples are dealt with by simply adding one more thing to the intrinsic value list. A moral theory should do more than just list what is good. That's the difference between cataloguing and theorizing. A theory should systematize an area in such a way that a deeper understanding is achieved. The worry about objective list theories is that this function of theory is sacrificed in order to avoid putative counterexamples.

It is a genuine worry. But this will not affect parsimonious lists that still strive to systematize morality. One way to do this is to try to find some other value that seems to have 'reductive potential' – that is, that seems promising as a basic, fundamental value. The perfectionist intuition appeals to achievement and genuine accomplishments. Happiness, of course, matters, but so do things like genuine accomplishments. Friendships and other close relationships, as well as genuinely significant personal projects, would all fall under the heading of the accomplishment category of value. This is one way to limit the proliferation of intrinsic value.

1.5 Maximization

The theory of the good is independent of the account specifying the right way to approach the good. Thus, consequentialist theories also need to provide an account of how to *approach* value. This completes the account of 'right action'. It isn't enough to simply know what the good is, one needs to have some account of production of the good, or promotion of the good, or honoring of the good in order to flesh out the account. Traditionally, consequentialists have held that the right action is the action that maximizes the amount of good relative to the alternative courses of action open to the agent at the time of action.

Yet this commitment to *maximization* of the good has been one of the more controversial features of utilitarianism. Offhand, it seems quite plausible to hold that if we ought to do good, we ought to do as much good as we can, given the relevant alternative courses of action we have to choose from. Indeed, this seems a requirement of rationality. Suppose that I hold up some money in both of my hands and ask you to choose a hand – you can have the money in whichever hand you choose. In one hand there is $1 and in the other hand there is $1,000. It would seem quite odd, and display a real lack of prudence, for you to choose $1 when you could have had $1,000 (on the assumption that money is something you want). Utilitarians note a moral analogue. If there are two choices of action, *a* and *b*, and if *a* is better than *b* all morally relevant factors considered, then morally I ought to do *a* rather than *b*. Failure here isn't a failure of prudence such as one sees in the money case, but it would be a moral failure since the good is not maximized. Consider a very simple case: Alice is walking home from work one day when she passes a lake. Two people appear to be drowning on the east side of the lake, and one person appears to be drowning on the west side of the lake. Alice is a strong swimmer, but she knows she will not have time to save all three, given how large the lake is and how long it would take to swim from one side to the other. She needs to decide to focus on one side of the lake. What should she do? Clearly, she should maximize the good that she can accomplish: in this case, she should choose the east side of the lake where two people are drowning and need her help. Proponents of maximization point out that if, in this case, she were to choose to save the one rather than the two, all other things being equal, she would be acting irrationally. She would be choosing the less good outcome in full knowledge and awareness that it is the less good outcome relative to her alternative of saving two lives. Given a focus on cases such as this, maximization of the good seems obvious, even something that seems rationally non-negotiable.

As plausible as this line of argument seems, however, it comes up against some fairly compelling problems. The major one is that it seems much too demanding. If we take this account of right action and obligation seriously, it would seem to wipe out an entire category of action – the supererogatory. Supererogatory actions are those that are 'good but not morally required'. So, for example, if I go out of my way to help someone carry his groceries home then I've done something that's nice, and that, intuitively, I am not morally obligated to do. But if this action maximizes the good in that it is better than the alternatives (walking home, getting a milkshake, feeding pigeons in the park, etc.), then I ought to do it in *any case*. It is my obligation. Thus, it would not in fact be supererogatory. And things get even worse when it comes to matching common-sense moral intuitions when we consider that the relevant alternatives are probably more likely to be things like: manning the phones at Greenpeace, writing a check to Oxfam, helping at the local soup kitchen, and so forth. If those are the actions that maximize the good, then those are the actions I ought to be performing. They are not 'supererogatory', they are *obligatory*. But to many it seems absurd to say that someone is morally bad, or has done something morally bad, when she buys a bagel for breakfast when she could have eaten cereal more cheaply and sent the balance of money to Oxfam. And this is one reason why many people reject utilitarianism. The problem seems even more profound when we consider people who do make significant sacrifices, but still fall short of the maximization standard. Consider the following:

> (M) Mike cares very deeply for other people, and each year he contributes 25 percent of his income to Oxfam, and related charities, in order to alleviate suffering in the world. Mike could contribute more. Contributing more would have a serious negative impact on his life-style, but his living conditions would still be far better than those of any of the people his money would go to help.

Because consequentialism demands maximization of the good, Mike is morally obligated to give more, even though he is giving far more already than most people give. It is true he could be doing more, but this is countered by the consideration that he is already doing more than his fair share in helping those in need.

It is this feature of consequentialism that is at least partly responsible for a famous line of criticism owed to Bernard Williams. The criticism goes something like this: utilitarianism, because it sets such a high bar for moral obligation, is an offensively moralizing theory. In eliminating, in effect, the category of the supererogatory utilitarianism leads to a domination of one's life by moral norms. Important projects that define a person's life become immoral, to be discarded in favor of a life spent helping those in need.

This problem holds the theory to be *moralizing*. 'Moralizing' is not a positive feature. It is a criticism. One form that moralizing takes mirrors the above criticism almost exactly. Some forms of moralizing involve agents treating supererogatory actions as obligatory.[13] A person who fails to do the best they can do morally has also failed morally. In making supererogatory acts obligatory the theory is illicitly requiring people to do more than they need to do in order to be decent human beings. But this problem overlooks a complication: it may be wrong to point out that someone has failed to maximize, and there may be very good moral reasons for recognizing a category of the supererogatory, even if one thinks that one's obligations are, strictly speaking, to maximize good rather than simply produce a certain less than optimal amount of the good. There may be extremely good effects to be achieved by praising people who do more than the norm, for example, even if what they do is still not optimal. In effect, this strategy

treats 'supererogatory' as a useful fiction. It is a fiction that is useful in motivating people to do better than they would otherwise do, and it is necessary
because we, as social beings, have a tendency to take our cues from those
around us. If the behavior of others sets the baseline for us, psychologically,
then it may just be a psychological fact about human beings that we need
an extra nudge – extra praise – to get us to act the way we ought to act in
the first place.

Further – and this is a theme to be explored more thoroughly throughout
the book – we need to be careful in spelling out the nature of the problem
itself. It may be that a good person, a person of good *character*, is not always
performing actions that maximize the good. Evaluation of character and
evaluation of action ought to be kept distinct.

A separate problem, but one that is often conflated with the standard
demandingness problem, is that utilitarianism seems to treat moral reasons
as *pervasive*. That is, given that for whatever action I perform there is a morally
significant alternative open to me, every single decision I make has moral
significance. Do I take the bus or walk home? Do I have a bagel or a veggie
burrito for lunch? Do I wear the red scarf or the green scarf? Even decisions
like these might be subject to questions of maximizing the good, and thus
be moral questions. And yet this seems completely absurd. Surely whether I
eat a bagel or a veggie burrito for lunch is morally neutral? Combined with
the view that moral reasons are *overriding* we do get a view like demandingness in a different way. Every decision we make is one where moral reasons
come to bear, and since moral reasons are overriding, the most morally
significant option will always take precedence. Thus, the theory doesn't
allow for morally neutral space in our lives.

To avoid demandingness some theorists have developed consequentialist alternatives to utilitarianism, such as *satisficing* consequentialism. On
the satisficing view, broadly speaking, the right action is the action(s) that
produces *enough* good.

There is some threshold of good such that if that threshold is met the
action qualifies as right. Going over that threshold would be supererogatory.
Michael Slote argued for such a position, holding that standard maximizing,
or optimizing, forms of consequentialism are strongly counterintuitive by
not allowing for supererogation and by placing too many demands on the
moral agent.

[I]f the person with special interest in India sacrifices that interest in order
to go somewhere else where he can do even more good, then he does

> better than (some plausible version of) satisficing act-consequentialism
> requires and acts supererogatorily. But optimizing act-consequentialism
> will presumably not treat such action as supererogatory because of its ...
> inordinately strict requirements of benevolence.[14]

One of the drawbacks to satisficing has seemed to be the very strong appeal maximizing has in the realm of prudence, as we noted above. But Michael Slote has argued that, actually, it can be *rational* for us to fail to maximize. Thus, the analogy doesn't really hold up. One example is that of wine choice: suppose that I prefer zinfandel to shiraz, though judge both to be perfectly satisfactory wines. On the maximization view it would be irrational for me to choose the shiraz, since I like zinfandel better. But Slote argues that this is mistaken – it is perfectly rational for me to pick the shiraz, as long as it is good enough. To the extent one finds this kind of case plausible, then, one might hold that maybe maximization of the good is not a requirement of rationality or morality. There can be moral choices that are good enough to count as 'right' even though they fail to maximize the good.

Non-philosophers have also attacked consequentialism for its commitment to maximizing. Gerd Gigerenzer argues that maximization "is typically out of reach in the real world" and that philosophers (among other benighted souls) tend to ignore this.[15] Because we are not capable of making all of the complicated calculations necessary for maximization, we are not in fact capable of determining the right action according to the consequentialist calculus. Thus, we need to opt for satisficing – for getting things 'good enough' – and, on his view, it is behavioral heuristics that can accomplish this. Heuristics offers shortcuts that really help us optimize performance. One example of such a heuristic is the recognition heuristic. The recognition heuristic enables judgers to make reliable inferences about a specific issue on the basis of very little data. Indeed, it is the lack of recognition exhibited by the judgers that enables them to make good inferences. One case Daniel Goldstein and Gigerenzer discuss is the following: a dozen Americans and Germans were asked "Which city is bigger, San Diego or San Antonio?" The Germans, who knew very little about American geography, were 100 percent correct in identifying San Diego as the larger city, whereas only two-thirds of the Americans answered correctly. The Germans were utilizing the recognition heuristic; in virtue of recognizing the name "San Diego" but not "San Antonio" they reasoned that San Diego would be the bigger city.[16] One can certainly assume that in moral cases heuristics come into play as well. All other things being equal, saving more lives is better than saving fewer, let's assume. Further, in very many circumstances one might not have enough information to know that 'all other things are equal'; and yet relying on a rule of thumb is what one ought to do – the efficiency costs associated with getting the extra information are too great, and in emergency situations one wouldn't have the time in any case. Of course, heuristics don't operate at the level of explicit rule application. But that they are good for us to use is a matter of deciding whether they really do help us achieve our aims, and the psychological research of Gigerenzer and his colleagues argues that, yes, they do.

While we agreed that heuristics are incredibly valuable in eliminating efficiency costs in moral action, Don Loeb and I responded by noting that this does not at all commit one to a satisficing view. Drawing such a conclusion involves a serious misunderstanding of consequentialism.[17] For example, this criticism ignores the distinction between decision-procedure and criterion of evaluation. It would only be a criticism if the theory held that one ought always to consciously try to maximize the good for any given single decision in isolation from other decisions one should be making. This is an absurd view and no consequentialist subscribes to it. Bentham explicitly denies it.

Further, even those who argue that agents must occasionally consciously apply the principle hold that agents ought to try to maximize what they expect to be the best outcome, given the available evidence. If one doesn't have access to the evidence, one certainly needn't try to use it.

They point out in addition that the satisficing alternative isn't plausible when one understands the role of efficiency, and the associated costs. The cases that make satisficing seem plausible, initially, are just cases of disguised maximization. Those in favor of maximization argue that the cases – such as Slote's wine case, above – are underdescribed. The standard problem is that the examples ignore efficiencies, which are extremely important in determining the true costs attached to an option. If I have to swim across shark-infested waters to get $1,000 then taking a safe, dry $10 might be the better option, even though $10 is much less money than $1,000.[18] This does not make one a satisficer, it simply recognizes that there are other costs aside from losing money. To use the shiraz case, it would be irrational to choose the shiraz under those circumstances. But what makes the case intuitively plausible is just that in many situations we find ourselves wanting to try something different – so there may be a novelty preference, I may want some variety, I may be bored with the zinfandel, and so forth. In which case the zinfandel is not really better.

Numerous writers have also pointed out that if satisficing – true satis-ficing and not disguised maximization – is used, then it will be justified to arbitrarily fail to do more good when one could have easily done it.[19] This is absurd. If I have a choice of saving one life, but could just as easily save two, then saying 'one is enough' does not exhaust my obligation. If one fails to save two in those circumstances then moral blame seems justified. It is interesting to note that this is a general problem for approaches that seek to limit one's obligations of benevolence, such as the obligation to rescue.

This latter issue also highlights the burden for the satisficer to try to determine what really is good enough. If we go the so-called 'fairness' route, then we end up with the problem alluded to above – seemingly arbi-trary failures to maximize are morally justified.

1.6 Scalar consequentialism

Another approach has been suggested in which act evaluation is scalar. There are two ways this approach can be developed: the eliminativist approach, which recommends eliminating 'right' and 'wrong' from moral discourse in favor of graduated judgments of 'good' and 'bad', or the non-elimina-tivist strategy which keeps 'right' and 'wrong' but understands those terms themselves as graduated. Mill sometimes seemed to speak as though he had this view. Consider his classic presentation of the utilitarian principle: "the Greatest Happiness Principle, holds that actions are right in proportion as they tend to promote happiness wrong as they tend to produce the reverse of happiness."[20]

A consideration against this proposal, however, is that 'right' doesn't seem to act like other scalar terms. For example, scalar terms are used twice to emphasize contrasts with other points on the relevant scale. For example, if I claim that my food is hot, a response might be, "But is it *hot* hot?" meaning something along the lines of "Is it really hot or just moder-ately hot?" This sounds odd with 'right'. If I claim to have done something right, and someone responds "But is it *right* right?", the response is odd-sounding. Either it is right or it isn't, period. Interestingly, however, the same oddity doesn't seem to carry over to 'wrong' – "But is it *wrong* wrong?" sounds better. For example, Alice jaywalks and then comes to the conclu-sion that what she did was wrong, and Bob responds "But was it *wrong* wrong?" meaning something like "was it really wrong or just a little bit?" What can we make of this? My hypothesis is that 'right' is not scalar, but 'good' and 'bad' are. Further, we sometimes use 'wrong' similarly to 'bad'.

The temptation to regard 'right' as scalar arises from the fact that we often intuitively conflate 'right' and 'good' in ordinary English.

Alastair Norcross is a consequentialist who opts for the eliminative strategy. He believes this approach can solve the demandingness problem for utilitarianism while at the same time retaining what is intuitively appealing about maximization. His theory is one in which the primary mode of evaluation of actions is as simply *better* or *worse* relative to the alternatives the agent is faced with. The most powerful argument used to bolster the view that 'right' is scalar is one that I will call 'the argument from negligible margins'. As Norcross notes, if one is not a scalar utilitarian, then one will have to hold that there is a threshold over which one's action is obligatory and under which one's action is wrong. His example involves the following: let's assume that we ought to give at least 10 percent of our incomes to charity. If this is the case, then 10 percent sets the threshold, so that if one gives at least 10 percent then one is doing the right thing, but if one gives 9 percent one is doing the wrong thing.[21] But the difference between 9 percent and 10 percent is not that large, and of course one can construct cases where the difference is quite negligible between performance and threshold. Yet the difference between right and wrong is pretty major. And this seems problematic for the threshold view. Instead, Norcross argues, we should reframe utilitarianism so that it is not a theory of the right but is instead simply a theory of the good and the better. There may be perfectly good *pragmatic* reasons for using 'right' and 'required' – just as there are perfectly good pragmatic reasons for setting a definite threshold for speed limits. But these thresholds don't themselves represent a deep moral truth about a moral property of a given action.

One problem for this line of argument is the assumption that the difference between right and wrong is always a profound difference. But this is not the case. Often an action is wrong, but the wrong is so trivial it hardly even warrants mention. If Roger takes a cheap ballpoint pen from Frank's desk he has done something wrong, but under normal circumstances the wrong is quite trivial. The right thing for Roger to have done is to refrain from taking the pen, but here the difference between right and wrong is not profound.

One interesting feature of Norcross' approach is that it makes a similar suggestion to that often (and mistakenly, in my opinion) attributed to Elizabeth Anscombe in "Modern Moral Philosophy."[22] That is, it offers an eliminativist thesis with respect to moral 'right' and moral 'obligation'. Anscombe famously argued that one of the problems with modern moral philosophy, including utilitarianism, is that modern theories made use of 'right' as an evaluative term cut off from its legalistic roots. For there to be prohibitions against certain actions there must be a prohibitor, a source of moral authority, and contemporary theories are lacking this since they have divorced 'right' from any theological understanding. Without God in one's theory as the source of moral authority, 'right' has no meaning; one can't, she claims, have a moral law without a moral lawgiver. She viewed the Kantian claim that we give the moral law to ourselves as absurd. Further, if one takes an alternative, virtue ethical approach, such as the one developed by Aristotle, one sees that the category of the moral – what we mean by 'moral' – doesn't map very well onto this. Many subsequent writers have disagreed with Anscombe on both points. But the suggestion that it might be possible to do ethics while jettisoning 'right' is something common to both her and Norcross.

Michael Slote noted that this maneuver distinguished some versions of virtue ethics from utilitarianism, since virtue ethics would suggest an elimination strategy (with respect to 'right') whereas the utilitarian offers a 'reductive' strategy – reducing the right to the good.[23] Slote wasn't pointing to an essential difference. He was pointing out, though, that the theories tended to be developed differently given the different foci. For virtue ethics, it was character traits, not actions, whereas for utilitarianism, it was actions rather than character traits. Numerous writers, however, have noted that these emphases are really historical artifacts.[24]

Eliminativism of this sort is radical, and open to numerous objections. One, which is quickly dealt with, is the objection that such a theory cannot guide action because it doesn't tell us what we must do to be morally good. It just tells us that some things are bad, and worse than others, and some things are good, and better than others, but that nothing is the right thing to do. Norcross can deal with this in similar fashion to the objective conse-quentialist. The primary role of the theory is to provide evaluative criteria; action-guidance is derivative. But eliminativism is drastic. Even contempo-rary virtue ethicists concede a role for 'right'.[25]

But this problem also afflicts the evaluative role. One of the reasons why we care about evaluation is that it can provide the raw materials for action guidance in that it can highlight the reasons that will make one action justi-fied within a set of alternatives. In hindsight, then, even if one rejects the view that the right moral decision-procedure actually incorporates those reasons as part of its content, the justifications can be used to give us reason to pick one decision-procedure over another. Further, this is useful because we want to know what the limits are. It is an illusion, really, that such a view will get us out of the demandingness problem if there is any sense at all in which we ought to do what is good. Of course, Norcross can claim it isn't a theory of what we ought to do, it's just a theory of what makes some actions morally better than others, and it is solely in virtue of their consequences that some actions are morally better than others.

A theory which identifies something as 'right' is sorting amongst the range of relevant alternatives. It is tempting to treat 'right action' as ambiguous between the subjective and objective senses – in some contexts, one might argue, we mean to focus on the agent's subjective states in contrast to the action's outcomes, and in other contexts it is the outcomes we focus on, given differing purposes. And it is quite true that 'right' is ambiguous between the subjective and objective senses. If William accidentally poisons his aunt when he is trying to get her a cup of sugared tea there's a sense in which what he did was wrong (he hurt his aunt) and what he did was not wrong (he did not intend to hurt his aunt). As will be discussed later in the book, the really interesting question is which sense, if any, is the primary sense of 'right' by which we understand and employ the other senses.

But we can *also* view 'right action' as a general term, like 'dog' or 'candy' or 'furniture'. 'Dog' is not *ambiguous* between 'collie' and 'Labrador'. Rather, 'dog' is a general term that refers equally well to collies and Labradors. There are different kinds of right action, just as there are different kinds of dog, candy, and furniture. It is interesting to ask what feature they have in common, which makes the term apply equally well to them. In the case of 'right action', the *objective* utilitarian, the one who ties 'rightness' to actual maximization of the good, notes that the core element of the theory is that rightness, or moral success, is tied to *outcomes*. All of the kinds of right action tie rightness to good outcomes in some way or other. That is the end of morally right action, just as knowledge is the point of belief. Justification isn't enough, though justification sets the boundaries for praise and blame. In Chapter 5 a more detailed account of treating the objective sense of 'right' as primary will be offered.

There is also strong *intuitive* appeal to seeing 'right' as a success term. This is one reason why maximization seems so plausible, at least initially. The right action in a given situation will be the best, and the best outcome is the one with the highest level of good. The natural comparison is with other success terms or concepts. The prudent action for me to perform at a given time is the one that *best* serves my interests, maximizing what is good *for me*, rather than total good. I may not be in a position to know which of the alternatives arrayed before me will have the best outcome. Indeed, it is precisely for this reason that people often diversify activities, like diversifying their portfolio of stocks. The idea in life, as in investment, is to guard against catastrophic loss. In the event of perfect knowledge this wouldn't be necessary. In retrospect, one might judge it better in the purely objective sense to have chosen the higher paying stock, A, over the lower paying B, though realize at the time of choice B looked best. And, despite what many critics of the objective view hold, this is action-guiding in a sense. These sorts of highly objective judgments of 'right' guide us in efforts to refine our decision-procedures, because we measure their success by how well we get good outcomes. We try to get more information that's relevant, and these judgments help us in the future to better identify what is relevant and what we should be looking for. But the reason we should be looking for more information, for refined decision-procedures and so forth, is that these things will help us achieve the outcome that really is the best, or get us closer to it. Subjective consequentialists confuse what is fundamentally important. Like many deontologists, they've chosen to put the cart before the horse, and identify moral quality with a procedure of some sort that the agent must conform to in acting rightly. While such subjective factors – at least ones that are indexed to the acting subject – do track praise and blame, they don't track rightness, or success.

This outlook does lead to oddities, but ones that under careful examination lose their oddity. There will be cases in which it is not practical to pursue what one knows to be the best. These include cases involving recognition of future errors on the part of the agent. To use an example adapted from one provided by Michael Zimmerman, suppose one has been invited to one's ex-wife's wedding, and knows the best thing to do is to go to the wedding and behave like a gentleman.[26] But one also knows that one is prone to drink too much at weddings, and this is likely to make one act foolishly. Should one go or not? No, one should not go, even though it would be best to go and behave well. It's just that one recognizes that isn't likely, and if that isn't likely, it doesn't seem like a practical alternative. There are at least two plausible ways to go with these sorts of cases. One can argue that we need to contextualize what counts as an alternative, and going to the ex-wife's wedding is not the best genuine alternative since one is likely to behave disastrously if one *does* go. What one ought to do, then, is not go, because it really is not the best *alternative*. The other way to go is to say that it is the best alternative, even if not a practical one because of the likelihood of one's future mistakes, and yet nevertheless one ought not to go to the wedding. This is interesting, because on this view one is saying that going to the wedding and acting well is the right thing to do, but one should not try to do it, even though one *knows* it is the right thing to do. This is a more radical split than the sort suggested before, supported by various examples including Norcross' dice example. On this view one holds 'right' to be an ideal, a *regulative* ideal. These sorts of cases also pose interesting issues about whether agents should consider what they think they *will* do, in preference to what they think they *can* do, in deciding how to act. This latter issue will be discussed in more detail in Chapter 6.

Uncertainty infects actual moral decision-making. Derek Parfit discusses the following example: 100 men are trapped in a mine following an explosion. There are two shafts, *A* and B. We know they are all in the same shaft, but we don't know which one. The chance they are in either one is fifty–fifty. Further, water is rising in the shafts, and there are three floodgates that would control the water. If gate 1 is closed, and the men are in shaft *A*, they are all saved. But if they are in shaft B they are all killed. If we close gate 2, the opposite is true, and if we close gate 3 we will definitely save ninety. This is similar to Frank Jackson's famous case regarding uncertainty about the best medicine to prescribe a patient, in that it seems clearly true on the objective account that closing either gate 1 or gate 2 is right, but we don't know which is right, but clearly closing gate 3 is wrong, since the outcome is suboptimal, and yet there is the strong feeling that that would be the right thing to do. But Jonathan Dancy helps out the objectivist here by noting that the ignorance of the best option itself should count as a reason, a morally relevant reason, that pushes one towards the third option.[27] When one acts one may need to choose an option one knows is not the best one, but not in cases where one knows what the best option is. *Given* that we don't know all the relevant facts, the right way to go is with gate 3. This is the right way to go, speaking loosely, even though one forgoes what one knows is the best option simply because one doesn't know the alternative that this the best option among those on offer. The objective account that goes further than Dancy is willing to go, though, holds that there is also a right way to go given all the facts, too, even ones that may be inaccessible to us. *Present* inaccessibility doesn't make them utterly normatively irrelevant, at least not in terms of what sorts of evaluations can apply to actions, motives, intentions and so forth. I may want to know what makes a star explode only because I'm worried about my star, and what makes my star explode may only be one little factor amongst others in the universe that influence other stars. I may never have access to any of those, but that doesn't affect the truth of claims that x and y in stars of type g make those stars explode. The truth is inaccessible, but it is out there. That's true of the objective rightness of an action as well.

But what the mine-shaft case shows is that in actual practice we should be considering the probabilities in deciding what to do. The expected utility associated with gate 3 is higher, so that's what we should go with. That is, one may still be doing the wrong thing, but one will be acting in a praise-worthy manner. Moving towards expected utility, as discussed earlier, is a move towards solving the applicability problem, but not within the account of 'right' itself.

Earlier I held that the account I would be arguing for is global, contextual, and objective. It is global in that the criterion for the moral quality of any feature of agency is consequences; it is objective in that the criterion does not necessarily appeal to the agent's actual psychology and, instead, appeals to what will in fact happen. I will now argue for the contextualist portion of the account. Alastair Norcross argues for contextualism for consequential-ists, arguing that to judge an action morally good in consequentialist terms we need to be able to compare possible worlds against a standard – the good action is the one that makes the world better, and making the world better is understood as making it better relative to some other possible world(s) that could have been brought about by the agent via alternative actions. But 'alternative' is understood as a 'relevant' alternative. Here's a case Norcross uses to make the point:

> *Perot.* Ross Perot gives $1000 to help the homeless in Dallas and I give $100.
>
> In most conversational contexts both of our actions will be judged to be good, because the appropriate alternatives will be ones in which we give no money. But consider again Perot's donation. Let's add a couple of details to the case: (i) Perot has a firm policy of donating up to, but no more than, $1000 per month to charity. (Some months he gives less than $1000, even as little as nothing at all, but he never gives more than $1000.) (ii) He had been intending to give $1000 this month to complete construction on a dam to provide water for a drought-stricken village in Somalia. As a result of Perot's switching the money this month to the homeless in Dallas, the dam takes another month to complete, during which time twenty children die of dehydration. Now it is not nearly so clear that we should say that Perot's action was good.[28]

The idea is that one's judgment of the action as morally good depends on what one takes to be the relevant point of comparison – that is, the alternative(s) used as comparison alternatives, or contrasts, in the given conversational context. I'm largely in agreement with this, and not simply for what counts as a morally good action, but also regarding what counts as the right action in a given context, relative to a given contrast. Thus, on this view, there is no action that is the right action *simpliciter*. Locutions such as "he did the right thing" are understood in a given conversational context. One of the interesting features of this sort of account of rightness, and moral goodness, is that when it comes to evaluating the truth or falsity of a moral claim one will need to pay attention to pragmatic factors. For example, while it is true that 'right' just *means* 'maximally good producing' on this account, "John performed the right action" then means "John did what was maximally good in his situation," so evaluating the claim as true or false will depend on what John's alternatives were, and what course of action we are contrasting with the one he actually selected. As in any other judgment of this sort, one can be mistaken. However, the claim is either true or false independently of what the judger believes. Contextualism is a kind of relativism, but not a pernicious kind of relativism, since the same standard of rightness and moral goodness applies across contexts. Contextualism with regard to moral claims is also independent of consequentialism.

This is not to abandon the objectivity of 'right', either. This issue is to be explored further in Chapter 5, but the account needs to be open to both objective and subjective senses of right, since both are clearly meaningfully used. The interesting question then becomes, which is primary? What makes the account objective is that the objective sense of right is taken to be explanatorily primary. What matters ultimately is what actually happens.

One interesting view has to do with whether 'right' claims are contrastive. So, does it make sense to say "p rather than q is the right action for A to perform"? Also, is there a contrast by which p would be the wrong action for A to perform? It seems that we can come up with plausible cases. Suppose that Marlene is being attacked by a homicidal burglar. She pulls out her gun, and has the options of (1) killing him; (2) wounding him; (3) firing a warning shot, and risk being killed herself; (4) not shooting at all, and being killed herself. In light of this scenario consider:

1   Marlene performed the right action in killing the burglar rather than letting him kill her.

2   Marlene performed the wrong action in killing the burglar rather than wounding him in the leg, which would have been sufficient to stop him.

This would mean that judgments of rightness are subject to how the issue is framed – that is, which contrast is conversationally assumed. This does not mean that it is impossible for an action to be right no matter the contrast. Rather, it means that there are judgments of 'right' which are sensitive to relevant contrasts and that this is a perfectly natural way to use the word.

An analogy might help. Let's say that 'right' means 'not wrong', just as 'flat' means something like 'not bumpy'. A table may be flat relative to a road, but not flat (i.e. bumpy) relative to the surface of a plate. It is possible that there is something that is flat relative to any normal contrast – perhaps the plastic surface of a computer chip. That, however, doesn't mean that 'flat' in many instances is not understood relative to a conversational, or contextually determined, contrast. Thus, a pragmatic claim about how we *use* the word 'right' should be distinguished from the metaphysical claim about what makes an action 'right'. The standard for 'right' is still actual production of the good. How we normally use the word 'right' in ordinary discussion will depend on contextual factors, which themselves may depend upon things like what our purposes are in making moral evaluations. Almost everyone agrees that our purposes are and should be sensitive to effects, in one way or another. But we may have serious practical interests at stake in limiting the scope of consequences we consider in evaluation in various ways. If we are worried about gun use, and the tendency someone might have to overreact to a perceived threat, we will focus on the contrast between Marlene killing her attacker and merely wounding him and stopping him. If we are worried about unsafe neighborhoods and how vulnerable people feel in the face of danger, we will focus on the contrast between Marlene killing the attacker and doing nothing at all.

1.7 Causing good and negative responsibility

Again, one core feature of consequentialism – and hence its name – is that moral evaluation and assignment of moral responsibility hinge on the consequences, or effects, of the agent's action, and that is generally understood as what the agent has *caused* to happen, relative to what other things he could have caused to happen. Consider these two claims:

(MR) The morally right action is the action that causally produces the best overall outcome.

And many other theories besides consequentialism also hold that:

(MC) Moral responsibility entails causal responsibility.

That is, if Mary did not cause an outcome, she is not morally responsible for the outcome. Consequentialism is generally taken to be committed to some form of both (MR) and (MC), and thus the notion of causation, or causal production, seems central to the theory.

However, this is not universal amongst those subscribing to some form of consequentialism. There is a complication. Even accepting something like (MC) as basic for moral responsibility, a distinction can be made between x being morally responsible for a and it being morally justified to hold x morally responsible for a. The latter is presumably, on the consequentialist view, constrained by (MR). This allows for the possibility that it may be morally permissible and even required that an innocent person (that is, someone who did not, for example, perform a) be held morally responsible for something he did not, in fact, cause. There is a classic case in the literature used to illustrate this point: suppose that a sheriff in a small town is confronted with the choice of (1) handing over an innocent person to a violent mob, who will kill him because the members of the mob mistakenly believe he committed a horrific murder or(2) keeping the man in protective custody, thus saving his life, but then not being able to stop the mob from rioting, and causing the deaths of twenty innocent persons in the ensuing riots.[29] On the straightforward act-consequentialist view it would seem that he ought to hand over the innocent person – it's one innocent life against twenty. Yet this seems horribly mistaken. And this returns us to the charge that the theory is incompatible with our notions of justice and desert. If we had a view of holding responsible, or praise and blame, that focused on the special effects – that is, the effects peculiar to the agent being held responsible – we could avoid much of the counterintuitive nature of this implication. Alice will only be moved by blaming her for a if she has, in fact, performed a.

However, we need to consider the general effects as well, and the hard cases are ones where holding responsible leads to good effects for others. The sheriff case can be taken as a dramatic example of this possibility. The intuition is that even if good effects are unquestionably brought about by the killing of an innocent person, it is still immoral, because the innocent person does not deserve to be killed. Saving the lives of other innocents, even very large numbers of them, does not make the action any more just or fair. If the prescriptions of consequentialism violate our norms of justice and fairness, then the theory is wrong, since it gives us incorrect guidance, and fails to properly evaluate the moral quality of actions.

This is a legitimate criticism, but we need to keep two issues distinct in making it. There is an assumption that if an action violates the norms of justice then the action is immoral. There is the further assumption that if an action is immoral it is impermissible. Both of these claims require further defense. First, one could well argue that many morally admirable actions violate norms of justice. The cases in which there is fairly deep agreement on this involve displays of mercy.[30] A thief may deserve ten years in prison as a penalty, but may be shown mercy in some circumstances – perhaps he has an ill mother, or children that rely on his support. Or, perhaps, the sentencing authority simply believes that he can benefit from the mercy in a morally significant way. But whatever the reason, failure to give him the punishment he deserves for his crime is not viewed as, necessarily, a morally bad thing.

Further, even leaving this issue aside, assuming it is immoral to violate the norms of justice, it doesn't follow that it is impermissible. It may be that a person's options are all 'immoral', at least intuitively, particularly when both options involve harming people who are innocent of any wrongdoing. Rosalind Hursthouse notes that in tragic dilemma cases we are unwilling to approve of an action even though we might all agree it was the action – amongst a range of extremely bad options – that the agent ought to have done. The *Sophie's Choice* dilemma is often used as an illustration. A woman must choose which of her children will be killed by Nazi soldiers, other-wise both are sure to die. Obviously, neither child deserves to die. Sophie must make a choice to avoid an even worse outcome, but it is not one that we can view as a good choice.

Noting the latter distinction, between immorality and impermissibility, seems the promising option for the consequentialist. Some actions that are immoral are nevertheless permissible, and even required, given that the other options open to the agent are worse. In actual practice, where effects are not clear, agents should err on the side of the norms that have the best track record in terms of promoting the good.

Many people view consequentialism as flawed because it is committed to *negative responsibility*. Roughly, this is the thesis that agents are morally responsible for the consequences of what they fail to do as well as the consequences of what they do. J. R. Lucas characterizes it this way:

> Often we do not act, and cannot be asked "Why did you do it?", but may sometimes be asked "Why did you not do it?" or "Why didn't you do something about it?" In those cases where we are obliged to answer this negative question, we have a 'negative responsibility'.[31]

To some consequentialists, and in particular utilitarians, putting it this way doesn't make much sense, because it trades on an illicit act–omission distinction. The consequentialist holds that we are responsible for the consequences of our actions – and inactions can always be described as actions of some sort – so that such a distinction doesn't make any sense. Suppose that Mary were to walk by an accident scene without stopping to give aid. Her action was to continue walking by the scene, and a consequence of her walking by is that she does not render aid to the injured persons. In this case, intuitively, her failure to do one thing by doing something else does render her to some extent morally (though probably not legally) responsible for the bad effects suffered by the injured people. It would be appropriate to ask, "Why didn't you do anything, at least call an ambulance?" or, to frame it in the positive terms "Why did you just keep walking instead of trying to help?" But regardless of how well founded one thinks the action–inaction distinction is, the holding of someone responsible under these sorts of circumstances is taken to involve a commitment to negative responsibility.

Clearly, as the case above illustrates, most of us have a commitment to negative responsibility to some extent. There are many cases similar to the one just described. On a much larger scale, Elie Wiesel has charged that the United States shares some blame for the extent of the Holocaust, since it failed to intervene to stop the Nazis at an earlier date. In a speech at the White House in 1999 he said of his time in the death camps:

> In the place that I come from, society was composed of three simple categories: the killers, the victims, and the bystanders. During the darkest of times, inside the ghettoes and death camps ... we felt abandoned, forgotten. All of us did. And our only miserable consolation was that we believed that Auschwitz and Treblinka were closely guarded secrets; that the leaders of the free world did not know what was going on behind those black gates and barbed wire; that they had no knowledge of the war against

the Jews that Hitler's armies and their accomplices waged as part of the war against the Allies.

   If they knew, we thought, surely those leaders would have moved heaven and earth to intervene. They would have spoken out with great outrage and conviction. They would have bombed the railways leading to Birkenau, just the railways, just once.[32]

And, he goes on to note, it turns out that they *did* know, and still did nothing to stop the slaughter, though it was in their power to stop some of it.

   With these sorts of cases a commitment to negative responsibility makes a great deal of sense, and seems to work in favor of the consequentialist. But there are several oddities that need to be explained. First of all, it would seem that it should be symmetrical between good and bad consequences. Yet this seems extremely counterintuitive. Let's assume that Carla could have prevented Robert from winning the spelling bee by spiking his orange juice and getting him drunk. But she doesn't do that. It does not seem credible to say that she shares responsibility for him winning the spelling bee just because she could have prevented it but didn't. Robert does not owe her. We need to explain the asymmetry. I have elsewhere argued that what the consequentialist should do is make a distinction between an agent *being* responsible for something, and it being justified to *hold* the agent responsible.[33] It may be that being responsible is just a simple causal notion. Being held responsible is the normative practice, and the justification for any application of this practice is determined by whether it produces the most good relative to not holding the responsible person responsible. It should be noted on this model that pragmatic factors enter into the picture at both levels. There may be pragmatic factors that determine how, exactly, we isolate a cause of a particular phenomenon. For example, as Hart and Honoré note, we don't attribute a fire to the presence of oxygen in the air, even though the oxygen is a necessary condition for the fire.[34] But once we identify a cause, we can ask a further pragmatic question — when that cause involves agency — as to whether it pays to hold the agent responsible. Clearly this is controversial. However, on my view it tracks our practices and gives a rationale for why we don't constantly engage in blame. Consider the case of Bob and Rob, two brothers. Bob is diligent, hardworking, and has internalized the right moral norms. Rob is a deadbeat who could not care less about moral norms. Their parents have found through painful experience that expressing blame to Rob does no good at all. It doesn't change Rob's behavior, and Bob doesn't need to profit from it. They've given up on expressing blame when it comes to Rob's behavior. Bob, on the other hand, is a different matter. On the rare occasions when he does something questionable, they will mildly blame him, and this seems sufficient to modify his behavior and attitudes. There is a difference, a critic will note, between blaming someone and expressing blame to someone. This is quite true. Rob's mother internally blames Rob when he does something bad, like stay out really late at night. But this is parasitic on the expression of blame she believes would be appropriate if only he would pay attention.

Another issue was raised by Bernard Williams. He found it particularly problematic that – as would seem to be the case if we buy into negative responsibility – an agent's level of responsibility for a bad outcome could be held hostage not just to unanticipated forces (which raises moral luck issues) but also to the goals and projects of other agents. This, he believes, makes a commitment to negative responsibility incompatible with the virtue of integrity, a virtue which enjoins agents to act on their deeply held principles and convictions, to remain true to themselves, so to speak, rather than true to some abstract principle which directs them to maximize the good.

For Williams the issue has to do with the significance of agency to moral responsibility. He would not deny that there are some cases where agents can be held morally responsible for outcomes if they fail to act. Suppose that a boulder rolls down a hill and threatens to crush a little baby. All Mary has to do is snatch it out of the path of the boulder to save its life, at no risk to herself at all. I believe that Williams would argue that she ought to save the baby and that if she doesn't she's exhibiting a terrible vice. The sorts of cases he has problems with are those where the requirement of negative responsibility would make one forgo a deeply held ethical value or project because of the effects of *someone else's* agency. Williams uses the well-known case of Jim and Pedro to illustrate the worry. Jim is a young man traveling through South America who is put into a very difficult situation. An evil dictator has ordered one of his minions, Pedro, to present Jim with an offer. The dictator has decided to make an example of local villagers. Either Jim kills one villager, or Pedro will kill twenty, including the one singled out for Jim to kill. Jim does not want to kill any innocent person. It goes against his deeply held values. Yet if Jim declines Pedro's offer is he morally responsible for the deaths of nineteen innocent people? Williams holds that whatever we think Jim should or should not do, if he does decline the offer and the twenty are killed, nineteen of whom could have been saved – Jim is in no way responsible. Pedro is the sole responsible agent. Holding Jim responsible would not be right.

> It is absurd to demand of such a man, when the sums come in from the utility network which the projects of others have in part determined, that he should just step aside from his own project and decision and acknowledge the decision which utilitarian calculation requires. It is to alienate him in a real sense from his actions and the source of his action in his own convictions. It is to make him into a channel between the input of everyone's projects, including his own, and an output of optimific decision; but this is to neglect the extent to which *his* actions and *his* decisions have to be seen as the actions and decisions which flow from the projects and attitudes with which he is most closely identified. It is thus, in the most literal sense, an attack on his integrity.[35]

A good deal of discussion has been given over to what exactly Williams was concerned with. Williams is not presenting counterexamples to the utilitarian definition of 'right action', since he thinks that it may well be the case that Jim ought to shoot the one to save the nineteen. Instead, he is arguing that if Jim does not shoot the one he should not be held responsible for the death of the nineteen, because it would be absurd to demand of him that he step aside from his own projects to prevent the bad outcomes generated by someone else's actions. Indeed, the point is deep. It is not simply that he should not be held responsible, it is, rather, that he is not morally responsible even though he knew full well he could have prevented the deaths of nineteen innocent people. A consequentialist could maintain that it might be counterproductive to hold him responsible even if he is responsible in virtue of his failure to act. While Williams' conclusion here seems counterintuitive to many, what it shows is that he is deciding to opt for the view that the demandingness of consequentialism is deeply problematic. Those who argue that Jim is responsible for the death of the nineteen if he fails to act are committed to the view (it would seem) that anybody who fails to save innocent lives when he or she could do so is also responsible for those deaths. Thus, very many people would be responsible for the deaths of people they could have saved through interventions they never made, for example. The theory seems to commit one to a view in which most people are responsible (at least partly) for horrifically bad outcomes that are the direct result of the actions of others. Thus, if famine in one part of the world is caused by poor land management of wealthy elites in that part of the world, and that mismanagement could be prevented by others but isn't, then they are responsible for the subsequent deaths as a result of the famine. There will be very many cases like this. Williams' worry is that to take the theory seriously we are committed to a life of intervention that precludes us from developing any meaningful life for ourselves. Of course, this conclusion has struck some writers as self-indulgent, or as due to a kind of squeamishness. Smart uses an analogy with the ordinary person's reluctance to cut into a human body, even when performing a life-saving operation. The reluctance is due to a kind of squeamishness that may, overall, be justified by consequentialism but interferes with performing the right action in specific cases.[36]

Timothy Chappell argues that to understand what Williams is concerned with we need to combine his discussion of negative responsibility with Williams' views on the nature of moral reasons. Williams believes that normative reasons, that is, reasons that justify one's actions, must be internal, that is, connected to the actual desires that the agent has. As Chappell puts it, Williams is committed to something like:

> (IRT) "nothing can count as a reason for me to act that is not either (a) in my range of motivations already, or (b) accessible by a sound deliberative route from what is already in my range of motivations."[37]

Thus, one's action is not justified by external reasons – that is, reasons not connected to one's actual motivations and desires.

Reasons internalism is quite a controversial view, and Chappell himself believes that Williams must be mistaken if this is really how to understand the integrity objection. This is because one could respond to the problem by noting that 'already existing motives' can be understood in a wide variety of ways, in such a way as to go beyond motives that are actually contained in my present motivational set. Clause (b) provides a good deal of scope in determining reasons outside of this set. For example, one might believe that human nature provides constraints on human beings that establish certain fundamental desires for all human beings, such as at least a bit of a desire for the well-being of others. This would be enough for the utilitarian.

Another way to take the argument reconstruction that Chappell proposes is to interpret Williams as arguing that reasons internalism shows that utilitarianism is practically unworkable, since it would violate 'ought-implies-can'. That is, it would require of agents that they perform actions that are motivationally impossible for them. If one is required to maximize the good, and yet one has no desire to do so, then it is not possible for one to maximize the good. If this is what is going on, though, the utilitarian has a ready response. The utilitarian holds that the right action maximizes the good amongst the options available to the agent. Indeed, if an action is not possible for the agent it is not an option.[38] But even more problematically, at least to those who do believe in normative moral theory, this kind of objection if seriously pushed by Williams cuts against a wide range of theories. Any theory committed to a view that motivation requires desire on the part of the agent will have the same problem, given that reasons internalism is true. A ready response would be to hold either that reasons internalism is not true, and that there are, indeed, external reasons, or to hold that normative ethics is simply addressing the issue of a standard for evaluating actions and isn't directly addressing the issue of how to get people to live up to that standard. That would become a separate, empirical issue. Both of these responses are promising. In the last portion of the book we will explore the issue of the separation of the standard of evaluation from the decision-procedure question.

However, Chappell argues that the integrity objection should be understood as the criticism that utilitarianism undermines *autonomous agency*. It not only demands that one maximize the good on occasion, it demands that one *always* maximize the good, and thus demands that one's actions always be constrained by the utilitarian calculus. This undercuts one's ability to choose based on one's own personal commitments. And this is just too demanding.

But the details of this criticism seem implausible. Chappell seems to view the utilitarian as condemning people to lives of *moral zombies*. Moral zombies are individuals, let's say, who behave as they do because someone else is acting for them, someone else is thinking for them. To make any sense of this, we'd need to view these individuals as shells inhabited by others. And, indeed, these are not autonomous agents. They aren't any sort of agent. On Chappell's view autonomous agency is very different from most other goods. No one can promote my own autonomous agency *except me*.

> The scope of my possible choices to help with, for instance, famine relief ... the scope of this sort of choice is not constrained by the fact that I am myself. But the scope of my possible choices to promote the existence of my own autonomous agency in pursuing certain freely chosen goals: this *is* constrained by the fact that I am myself. If my entire life course was micromanaged for me by someone else, as lives are on Nozick's Experience

> Machine, my life would lack meaning, just because it would not be me living it. Anyone at all can give to famine relief; but I alone am responsible for whether *I* have a meaningful life.[39]

This criticism involves a misreading of the experience machine thought experiment. The person in the experience machine can fully well make choices; it is just that those choices do not lead to veridical experiences. The person in the experience machine is exercising autonomy, it is not like *spectating*. Chappell's sense of autonomy is the sense that philosophers use to talk about agents who are deceived lacking autonomy — there is a sense in which that is true, but another sense in which it is not true. The person who is deceived does make choices; it is just that those choices are not the same ones he or she would make when fully informed. This is unfortunate, but it seems a gross overstatement to say that such a person's life would lack any meaning at all because it isn't 'me' living it. Deceived people are still living their own lives, just not (barring unusual circumstances) optimal lives.

Yet negative responsibility would seem to commit us to holding Jim responsible, that is, partly responsible, because he could have prevented the bad outcome and yet did not. The key factor affecting intuitions seems to be *intervening* agency. Imagine the scenario somewhat differently. Suppose that the doomed person in the situation has a terrible infectious disease and that if Jim does not quarantine him then he will innocently spread the disease to others and they will die along with him. However, in isolating him Jim is denying him any medical care, which we normally believe people are entitled to. Here it is a disease, and not a person, who is causing the preventable harm. Here, if Jim fails to act then there is a greater tendency to hold him responsible, unlike the case where Pedro — another agent — has set up the dilemma for Jim. We cannot blame diseases, but we can blame Pedro.

Lucas echoes this intuition: "if he [referring to Jim] refuses, and the guerrillas carry out their threat, he is not automatically and necessarily answerable for what happens. He has not killed anyone. The deaths are due entirely to the guerrillas' actions, not to his inaction. The chain of causal responsibility is broken by their autonomous action".[40]

Given these observations, we can make the interpretive claim that the objectionable commitment to negative responsibility holds one responsible for outcomes one could have prevented even in cases where another person's agency was the proximate positive (rather than negative) cause of the bad outcome. Thus, it would be claimed, if consequentialism holds Jim responsible for the death of the nineteen villagers, simply because he could have prevented their deaths, then that's objectionable because it violates his integrity, by calling on him to do something that he thinks is terrible, and because there is another agent who is the real positive cause of the bad outcome of the nineteen being killed – the actual shooter. If one pursues this line, holding that negative responsibility is objectionable only when it both involves a violation of integrity and involves another agent in the way described above, one can limit the scope of the objection, and keep some of the intuitive plausibility of the claim that we do sometimes hold people responsible for what they don't do.

Let's then consider a variation on the boulder case to illustrate. In Boulder II the boulder has not slid down the hill after a rainstorm loosens the dirt around its base. Instead, an evil person has pushed it down the hill in an attempt to crush the baby. If Mary stands by and fails to pull the baby from its path, is she partly responsible for the baby's death? I think, intuitively, we'd say yes – but note that pulling babies out of the path of danger is not something that constitutes a violation of integrity. As described so far it doesn't call for Mary to act against a deeply held value or forgo an important project. So this case doesn't conform to the criteria set out above. But consider a closely related case: the same as Boulder II, but Mary is in the midst of putting the finishing touches to an ice sculpture that would showcase her talents and lead to all kinds of artistic opportunities for her. If she stops sculpting, though, to go save the baby the sculpture will melt, ruining her hopes and aspirations. Here is a case in which she is asked to forgo a significantly important project in order to save someone's life. While maybe not as compelling as Boulder II, this case – Boulder III – still seems one in which Mary, if she doesn't set aside her task and save the baby, shares some responsibility for the baby's death. It also seems, to me, at any rate, that here the agency situation doesn't make much difference. Mary is to some extent responsible whether the boulder slipped or was pushed.

What should we do? Should we take agency into consideration? There is one direct and compelling consequentialist argument for taking agency into consideration. Failure to do so might provide encouragement to those other people who would act badly. Suppose a terrorist threatens to blow up a school unless his demands are met. In any particular case those demands may be minor – for example, a demand to read a rambling, insane manifesto over the radio. Here, if the broadcaster refuses permission and the school children are killed, then some may well hold him responsible for the deaths of the children – even though the broadcaster feels that providing air time to terrorists is wrong. The FBI has rules that strongly discourage granting the demands of terrorists, even relatively harmless demands, because they feel that it might encourage terrorism and lead to escalated acts of terrorism. If prospective terrorists see that such behavior is rewarded, this provides additional incentive, and what we should be doing, to improve the long-term consequences, is to discourage such behavior.

Interestingly Williams seems to argue that it is utilitarianism's detachment from the reality of human experience in the form of our projects and values that creates this problem with integrity. But Williams' Jim and Pedro case works only because it is detached and Williams is considering this case from an objective point of view. Should Jim decline the offer because the deaths are Pedro's responsibility, and not his? This sort of reasoning is cold comfort to a parent imagining what to do when kidnappers demand ransom. "Oh, it's not my fault, it's the kidnappers'!" doesn't seem psychologically realistic. If we do think people should not pay ransom it is usually because of consequences – ransoms encourage other kidnappings and the overall problem is made bigger. This seems a mistake. Relying on others to be good agents may be a way of respecting them, but it will lead to very poor outcomes and a good deal of harm to innocent people.

Further, Williams himself has a demandingness problem, given that he takes integrity seriously. Elizabeth Ashford has pointed out that the integrity objection is a double-edged sword for him. She argues, convincingly, that any plausible account of integrity needs to be objective. That is, if one's integrity revolves around what value commitments agents possess, regardless of their objective normative worth, then the account is deeply flawed. Many writers have also noted that if we view integrity as value neutral in the objective sense, then we will end up having to view people with terrible values as nevertheless people with moral integrity, as long as they are truly committed to those values. This seems very counterintuitive. If one accepts that integrity needs to be tied to *genuine* values, commitments with objective value, then, Ashford argues, an agent with integrity is committed to a self-conception that exemplifies real value. In the world we actually live in people live in conditions of desperate need while others live lives of leisure. This is really the root of demandingness. Ashford argues that in the world as we actually experience it, the objective integrity of the affluent is threatened by the demands placed on them by utilitarianism, which holds that one has an obligation to trade off relatively insignificant benefits, such as enrollment in an art class, for the sake of saving lives. But, then, isn't it just true that trade-offs do seem appropriate in these circumstances? Ashford writes:

> Utilitarianism's acknowledgement that in the current state of the world agents' objective integrity is inevitably threatened is, I suggest, entirely appropriate. When agents' pursuit of their ground projects conflicts with their saving others' vital interests, this poses a problem for agents' leading integrated good lives which should not be viewed as resolvable. Those facing extreme poverty have a claim that their vital interests be met which cannot be ignored.[41]

Her point is that even if we decide to not live lives devoted to the well-being of others, we should feel morally compromised. Developing my artistic talents may be important to me, but surely not as important as someone's life.

It seems clear that there is something to the commitment to negative responsibility. An agent's level of moral responsibility for actions can be held hostage to the goals and activities of others. But it does seem that if we must factor in immoral agency we must also factor in moral agency in determining responsibility, and this could lead to other counterintuitive results. Suppose that Roger realizes that if he doesn't donate $1,000 to Oxfam, Doug will. Rather than donate the $1,000 himself, he refrains. Does he share in responsibility – moral responsibility – for the good brought about by Doug's contribution? The asymmetry, though, as noted earlier, can be accounted for through pragmatics. That is, we have stronger incentives to prevent harms being committed by those actually tempted or inclined for some reason to commit them, and these are the ones that we tend to focus on.

One major difficulty for consequentialism, though certainly not exclusively for consequentialism, is to provide some principled way to limit the scope of negative responsibility. One strategy that could be pursued is to suggest that there is no sense of moral responsibility except as "that which it would be appropriate to praise or blame someone for." Within a consequentialist framework the appropriateness of praise and blame is determined by outcomes, rather than some independent notion of desert. The objective consequentialist might hold that we are responsible for myriad outcomes in performing a given act, but it is a separate issue to determine which things we should be praised or blamed for doing. The agent's states of mind – actual rather than idealized – are relevant here. The objective consequentialist is free to hold that the agent's states of mind are extrinsically good or bad depending on the outcomes they are causally correlated with. We should praise a person with good intentions because doing so produces the better overall outcome.[42] Another factor might be cost to the agent: if someone normally is not tempted to do something bad, then refraining from doing it costs them little or nothing. There's no point in the praise, then.

In the Jim and Pedro case, one possible approach is to hold that if Jim does not kill the one to save the other nineteen he has done something wrong, but not something we would blame him for. In this case the reason might be that we need to make a distinction between character evaluation and act evaluation. So, the action does produce a non-maximal outcome, but it may also be true that it's a good thing, by and large, that people cannot bring themselves to kill others. This inhibition is good for people to have for consequentialist reasons. The disposition to avoid killing the innocent, then, may be one that is systematically productive of good outcomes. This is completely consistent with the view that there's no particular decision-procedure that's the right one for all contexts − the correct decision-procedure employed by the agent will likely vary from context to context, depending on what brings about the best outcome. This is also completely consistent with the view that the moral agent − though responsive to the right sorts of reasons − does not *consciously* think in terms of those reasons. These reasons, for example, may be reflected in moral commitments of the agent, beliefs that are dispositional for the agent, only articulated, if at all, when the agent is explicitly asked or prompted to provide reasons.

Chapter summary

This chapter had two broad tasks: canvassing accounts of value and approaches to value. Each of these issues is of key importance in a consequentialist theory. The classical utilitarians adopted a hedonistic account of intrinsic value as well as a maximization approach to value, but other consequentialists have departed from this template. In this chapter the alternatives are critically discussed. For example, some writers have argued that instead of hedonism, we should view value in terms of desire satisfaction, which may or may not be pleasurable. Some consequentialists argue that maximizing the good is too demanding, and that, instead, consequentialism should simply require agents to satisfice − that is, produce an amount of good that is 'good enough'.

Further reading

Wayne Sumner, *Welfare, Happiness, and Ethics* (Oxford: Clarendon Press, 1996).

On the issue of maximizing, and defending robust consequentialism, Shelly Kagan's *The Limits of Morality* (New York: Oxford University Press, 1989) is a classic. He demonstrates how full-bore maximizing consequentialism seems to follow from fairly uncontroversial assumptions.

On satisficing: Michael Slote, *Beyond Optimizing: A Study of Rational Choice* (Cambridge, MA: Harvard University Press, 1989).

On scalar consequentialism: Alastair Norcross, "The Scalar Approach to Utilitarianism," in *The Blackwell Guide to Mill's "Utilitarianism,"* ed. Henry West (Malden, MA: Blackwell, 2008).

On the integrity objection: Elizabeth Ashford, "Utilitarianism, Integrity, and Partiality," *Journal of Philosophy* 97 (2000), 421–39.

3

AGGREGATION

Henry Sidgwick pointed out that the classic version of utilitarianism, the version developed by Bentham and Mill, is underdetermined in a variety of ways. Later, John Rawls would pick up on this theme to criticize utilitarianism for failing to take seriously the value of fairness and equality in its distribution schemes. The kind of underdetermination we look at in this chapter has to do with aggregation. That is, how are we to understand the maximization standard? First, do we try to produce the greatest amount of *total* good or do we instead try to produce the greatest amount of *average* good? Some later writers, such as J. J. C. Smart, have felt this was not, in practice, a crucial distinction since both ways of aggregating outcomes would recommend the same practice in the end. This is not plausible, however, for reasons we will discuss.

Second, even if this issue is resolved, there is the further issue of unfair, unjust, or inequitable distributions. This was the issue that primarily concerned John Rawls in his famous criticism of utilitarianism in *Theory of Justice* when he wrote of the utilitarian approach to justice:

> The striking feature of the utilitarian view of justice is that it does not matter, except indirectly, how this sum of satisfactions is distributed among individuals any more than it matters, except indirectly, how one man distributes his satisfactions over time. The correct distribution in either case is that which yields the maximum fulfillment.[1]

This feature of utilitarianism, in turn, leads to what Rawls termed a denial of the 'separateness of persons'. On his characterization this is accomplished by the utilitarian considering the maximizing strategy from the point of view of a single person who seeks to maximize the good – ideally, an impartial, sympathetically engaged spectator. Such a spectator will determine rules of justice on the basis of what rules maximize the good, even if that means the good is distributed unequally amongst the persons in that society:

> This view of social cooperation is the consequence of extending to society the principle of choice for one man, and then, to make this extension work, conflating all persons into one through the imaginative acts of the impartial sympathetic spectator. Utilitarianism does not take seriously the distinction between persons.[2]

This sounds very bad. However, it may just boil down to the utilitarians' proper recognition that the desires of one person matter no more or no less than the desires of any other person. On this score, writers like Will Kymlicka believe that utilitarianism actually has a rather nice, built-in, notion of equality which leads to an intuitive conception of just distribution of goods.[3]

1.1 Average vs. total

Offhand, people are inclined to favor the total good view. This view holds that the right action maximizes the total amount of good. Thus, given the agent must choose between saving one life and saving two, all other things being equal, the right action would be to save two since that increases the total amount of happiness. It would do nothing to increase or decrease the average amount (again, given that the existing happiness levels of the individuals were the same), and so it would seem odd to favor average consequentialism. On the other hand, if we opt for the total view, we get other problems since the total view isn't committed to any particular pattern of good distribution. Consider the following scenarios:

A   1,000 people at 100 units of happiness each = 100,000 units of total happiness.

B   100,000 people at 1 unit of happiness each = 100,000 units of total happiness.

On the total view it looks as if A and B are equally good patterns of distribution, but this seems wrong. A seems much better than B because the people in A are happier – far happier – even though there are fewer of them. This judgment can have far-reaching practical implications, particularly when it comes to formulating public policy. If one agrees that A is better than B, then one is rejecting the total happiness view that would hold them to be equivalent. One would opt for policies that increased the level of happiness (i.e. average) rather than the amount (i.e. total). In practice this might consist in opting for family-planning policies that would discourage people from having more children, for example, and focus instead on increasing the happiness level of fewer children. So, there *does* seem to be a practical difference. And this is just one case.

Derek Parfit has detailed some very plausible scenarios in which the total/average distinction can have enormous significance, building on the intuition developed above. The following cases are Parfit's examples.[4]

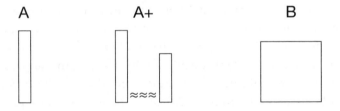

In A, everyone is living a good life – lives that are well worth living. A+ is like A except that we've added another group of people who, while still happy, are not as happy as those living in A. The two populations are separated by a body of water, let's suppose, so they don't know about each other, and thus aren't aware of any inequality. It seems highly plausible that A+ is certainly no worse than A even though the added population brings down the average level of happiness in that world. Thus, this seems to favor the total version. On the other hand, compare B with A+. B has the same number of people as A+, but the average welfare is slightly higher than that in A+, though lower than that of A. Intuitively, it would seem that B is better than A+ (same number of people, higher average welfare, and equality). However, B does not seem better than A, though, given the reasoning we employed it would seem to follow that B is better than A. If we accept that B is better than A, then we will be led to what Parfit calls the "Repugnant Conclusion" – a world where there are very, very many more people than in A, at a level of welfare that is also minimal: lives barely worth living. A preference for quantity over quality would seem to lead to this, and this seems very wrong. Isn't it better to have fewer very happy people than large masses of barely happy people? Much family-planning policy rests on the intuition that it is better to control population in favor of increasing, or at the least, preserving, a good standard of living for members of the population as a whole. In any case, these examples show that in principle there is much at stake in deciding between total and average consequentialism.

Some have argued that one way to solve the problem is to restrict moral considerability to those persons who actually exist or have existed or will exist. This is an example of what some theorists term 'the person-affecting' view of welfare, since it holds that welfare is attached to persons – a state is better or worse for actual individual persons rather than with respect, also, to possible people. We can call these theorists *welfare actualists*. The basic idea is that while the choices an individual makes certainly affect who is brought into existence – for example, should Stella have a baby now or wait for a couple of years? – neither of the merely possible babies has moral considerability. Only the one that actually will exist does. These individuals may not be individually identifiable ahead of time, but that does not mean that they lack moral considerability. Further, this approach has the nice feature of explaining why people don't do anything wrong when they decide *not* to have children. All of us have very many *possible* children, but we choose to bring only some of them into *actual* existence. Given this view of welfare, combined with the consequentialist view of rightness, it would turn out that the right action is the one that has maximally good positive effect relative to the interests of only actually existing persons (people who have existed, do exist, and will exist). This seems highly intuitive since, if someone is merely possible, and will not actually exist, why should I consider that person's welfare in my deliberations about how to act morally? Why should those phantom interests weigh at all in evaluating any action that I perform?

Unfortunately, this approach has its own set of problems. For example, Caspar Hare notes that it has a serious problem with the following case, adapted from Jan Narveson's work:

> *Childless George* – George passes up an opportunity to conceive a child who would, George has every reason to think, be relentlessly miserable from the start to the end of his or her sorry little life. By doing so, George imposes some small cost on actual people.[5]

It seems that George has done the right thing by not having a miserable child, even though he has had a negative impact (even though extremely minor) on actual persons. Some writers, like Josh Parsons, argue, however, that even though George did not do the right thing, he still deserves some moral credit for avoiding the performance of a really bad action.[6]

One might think, though, that this kind of case raises a really fundamental problem for this approach. The problem is that we really think that modal considerations – that is, considerations of what might have been, or what could be the case, for example – are relevant to moral evaluation. The actualist seems to be denying this.

The intuition that possibilities matter is supported by the fact that we also think that some matter more than others. The extent to which we judge a possibility as 'realistic' or 'far-fetched' affects our judgment of an action. If Sandra's driving drunk only had a very slim chance of harming someone (since she was driving out in the country, where there were almost no people about) as opposed to a significant chance (she is driving in the city, where many other people are driving), we will judge it less harshly even though in both cases no actual person was harmed. It would seem that if harm to actual persons is what determines the moral quality of the action, then both acts are equally bad, morally.

There is a response the actualist can make here, however. The actualist can hold that some possibilities are relevant, as long as they are possibilities with respect to actual persons. Sandra driving drunk away from people is less bad than Sandra driving drunk in a densely populated area, because the imposed risks on actual people are very different.

More difficult cases are the ones where risks seem to be imposed, but not on any particular people. Still, the actualist can hold that the harm is inflicted on *classes* of actual people so as to produce a worse state of affairs.

There are some writers who deny that the 'repugnant' conclusion is really repugnant, or, at least, something that it would be immoral to bring about. Some have argued that, though the conclusion does seem highly counterintuitive, the problem is with our intuitions themselves. We mistakenly think that a life barely worth living is actually a bad life, when it is not – it is a life that still contains a higher level of happiness than unhappiness. It is not a terrible life at all.[7] Once people are clear about this, then the conclusion seems a bit more plausible. This is still somewhat counterintuitive, however, in that most people in practical deliberation will opt at some point for fewer people with happier lives. Those who favor the deflationary option will likely claim that the counterintuition confuses different sorts of goods. It is prudentially good for people to opt for increasing averages, rather than to opt for a shallower but broader distribution. But, they will claim, the *morally* best option is to distribute happiness more broadly. There might be something to this observation. However, the intuition that broad and shallow distribution is morally best is not shared by a disinterested party, necessarily. If an agent has to decide how to give money away, for example, money that he will not himself be eligible for, he might quite reasonably prefer to make a bigger per person impact rather than distribute a dollar each to thousands of people or a penny each to even more people.

Various compromise options have been discussed in the literature as well. One compromise is to hold that once average utility gets beyond some 'critical level' then we are free to promote total utility in terms of adding more persons to the population who at least have a level of happiness at or above whatever the critical level turns out to be. This maneuver mirrors moves made in political philosophy on the issue of just distributions. Once 'basic needs' are met for everyone, then we can switch from increasing average to increasing total. Aside from brute conformity with our intuitions, there is little to recommend this strategy.

Another option is to hold that given we are willing to include psychological factors in our account of well-being, which seems highly plausible, it's worth noting that there is evidence that a person's level of subjective happiness varies according to the person's perception of how they fare *relative to others*.[8] Elder Shafir, Peter Diamond, and Amos Tversky asked a group of people to consider the cases of two people, Carol and Donna. They both graduated from the same college and they both went into the same profession, working for publishing firms. As they laid out the story, Carol started out at a yearly salary of \$36,000 in a company where the average starting salary was \$40,000 a year whereas Donna started out at a yearly salary of \$34,000 at a company where the average starting pay was \$30,000. Thus, Carol has the higher absolute salary, Donna has the higher salary relative to her coworkers. Shafir *et al.* then noted the following:

> When we asked subjects who they thought was happier with her job situation, 80 percent of respondents (N = 180) chose Donna, the woman with the lower absolute salary, but with the better relative position. Furthermore, when we asked a second group of respondents (N = 175) who they thought was more likely to leave her position for a job with another firm, 66 percent chose Carol, the one with the higher absolute salary but the lower relative position.[9]

They also noted that when people claimed that they themselves would opt for the higher absolute salary, they also seemed to recognize that their job satisfaction would be higher where their salaries were comparatively better. The phenomenon of relative deprivation is well known. We do tend to modulate feelings of well-being relative to our perceptions of the well-being of others. For some writers, this is key to understanding the nature of poverty.[10] Poverty can exist independently of starvation (though starvation entails poverty), since poverty is a matter of relative deprivation whereas starvation involves 'absolute dispossession' of what one needs for sustenance. This captures the intuition that a person can live in poverty in the United States, even though not actually be starving to death. The poverty consists in living well below the normal standard of living for the population. That may even be above the normal living standard for other populations, and still count as poverty in the United States. Well-being, then, involves subjective factors as well as objective ones such as enough goods to satisfy our physical needs. What may lend credibility to the view that the repugnant conclusion, properly understood, isn't all that repugnant may be the insight that, as described, it just seems psychologically very boring for those involved, those who, as typical human beings seem to do, derive a measure of happiness from ranking themselves better than others. This ranking can occur, of course, along a wide variety of parameters. Indeed, those who would opt for the job that paid more in absolute terms, but less in relative terms, and yet note that their job satisfaction would probably be lower, are likely to have the view they have because they recognize that the extra money will enable them to achieve a higher level of satisfaction along some other parameter – such as stamp collecting, travel, or what have you.

The repugnant conclusion is not the only problem for the total view, however. It seems fundamentally incompatible with the value of fairness. John Rawls famously maintained that utilitarianism suffers as a theory by losing sight of the distinction between persons when it comes to aggregating goods. And this will lead to unfair distributions of goods. The average consequentialist seems to have an advantage here since improving average utility would involve bringing up the average in a population. None would be made to suffer unduly in order to disproportionately benefit someone else. Consider the following distribution scheme:

A*   100 people at 300 units, 10,000 at 40 units = 700,000 units.
B*   8,000 people at 80 units = 640,000 units.

In A* there are 100 extremely happy people who live off the labor of the rest of the population, 10,000 people who are decently happy but who are living lives that put them under the control of the 100 in the 'elite' class. In B* there is no such hierarchy. There are 8,000 people who are all pretty happy, twice as happy as the bulk of the population in A*. The society is egalitarian, no one who is able to work lives off the labor of anyone else. Still, A* has more happiness in total than B*. Yet, B* seems morally better. It seems morally better because it seems wrong for some people to gain their happiness by exploiting others. Yet, strictly speaking, total utilitarianism doesn't seem to be able to handle this sort of case. The theory is supposed to give us guidance about what's best, as well as a criterion to evaluate distribution schemes. But, in the case of A* and B*, it seems completely mistaken.

One way to handle this case is to hold that it isn't so much an issue for aggregation of the good as it is an issue for how we specify the nature of the good. Classical utilitarianism was committed to hedonism, but later forms of consequentialism are much more expansive on the issue of intrinsic good. One might hold that 'fairness' or 'autonomy' are goods, and that what's wrong with A3 is that the happiness of some is gained at the loss of autonomy of others, and that this is actually an intrinsically bad factor that has to be weighed in the balance. There are two basic problems with this approach. One is that, though it can handle this particular case, the critic simply has to reformulate the case in a different way to make the same basic objection. Suppose that we have a society in which the autonomy of the few is enormously enhanced by violating the autonomy of the many ever so slightly, for example, and yet total autonomy is greater than that in a more egalitarian scheme. Another problem is one mentioned in Chapter 2. This general strategy strikes many as ad hoc. If the consequentialist approaches every putative counterexample by simply expanding the class of intrinsic goods to accommodate the cases, then the theory risks losing any prescriptive force.

Every individual's happiness matters, and no one's happiness matters more than anyone else's. Importantly, we need, as a heuristic, to count all persons the same in terms of providing benefits. Why? What will happen if benefits get awarded disproportionately is that people will adjust their demands accordingly – they will claim to actually like ice cream more, or derive more happiness from luxury items, than is the case. Demands on the benevolence of others will escalate. Treat everyone the same, even if some really do like ice cream more than others, and one avoids this problem.

Thus egalitarian distribution schemes are justified on the basis of conse-quentialist considerations, even though what would be best under ideal circumstances is just to increase total happiness.

However, critics would note that this doesn't avoid all fairness issues. Don't people who work harder deserve more goods, even if those goods could go to somewhere else to increase average happiness? The crux is that critics claim that one can't have a pure consequentialist theory that is respon-sive to deeply held intuitions about fairness and equality. Instead, the best one can hope for (if one cares to accommodate these intuitions) is a kind of hybrid theory that holds that maximizing the good is a kind of default option, but that it is constrained by individual rights, or entitlements; and/or that even if there is a default requirement to maximize the good, that is offset by permissions to fail to maximize under certain circumstances – for example, when the well-being of friends and family members is at stake.[11] Indeed, there is a fairly common perception that pure consequentialism is incompatible with the norms of friendship and love, since these norms are by their very nature partial rather than impartial.[12] David McNaughton and Piers Rawling argue that the simple consequentialist can't hold that there are such things as benefits, that is, states of affairs that are good for x, but not good for y, for example, without having a problem explaining how it is that we have reasons to benefit the near and dear rather than promote the overall good.

But this is a mistaken criticism. Partial norms of love and friendship that involve showing preference for the 'near and dear' can be justified along consequentialist lines. These norms would, in turn, give rise to partial reasons to promote the good of specific individuals, even if, on a specific occasion, the benefit to the individual could not be cashed out in terms of promoting the overall good. A parent has a reason to benefit her child by bringing about states of affairs that are good for the child, even if those states of affairs may make someone else worse off, and, indeed, may reduce the overall good. But this framework is not itself a primitive, in no need of justification. Its justification is consequentialist.

For example, Frank Jackson uses what he calls a 'sector argument'.[13] Consequentialism is pragmatic. It is sensitive to psychological reality. One feature of human beings that is a given is that they fall in love, have families, and develop friendships. These relationships are instrumentally valuable in that they are crucial to human happiness, given the facts of our psychology. But these relationships are also important normatively in that given we are finite beings – which we clearly are – spreading benevolent concern too broadly is ineffective. What is effective is focusing our benevolent attentions on a relatively small group of individuals to whom we become particularly attached. The goodness of these relations consists not only in their being just intrinsically satisfying to people, which they are, but also in terms of consequentialist efficiency.

We can consider analogies with other sorts of focusing behavior. To maximize performance of a task it may be necessary to screen out 'background noise', so, in order to concentrate on a conversation at a cocktail party, people develop habits of filtering out extraneous noise, ignoring what isn't actually part of the conversation.[14] The analogy would be that to effectively pay attention to friends, family members, and so forth – that is, others who are crucial to our social environment – we need to focus on them and learn to ignore or attentively, anyway, withdraw from others. This needn't be an explicit process, either, where the agent is consciously trying to filter. It is a response to our environment that prevents us from moving about in a distracted manner. This is just a feature of our psychology. The attentive agent may or may not practice filtering in recognition of its value in helping us navigate the world effectively.

It is important to emphasize that few consequentialists would argue that agents who are in love, for example, think in instrumental terms, or think in terms of how important it is for people to focus benevolent concern. That is not what motivates them, and it is not what *ought* to motivate them. But it *is* what morally *justifies* that concern. The critics who make this attack tend to treat the justification conditions as parasitic on motivation, which many consequentialists reject. Sidgwick pointed out that motivation and justification come apart. Motivation deals with a cause of the action being evaluated, but the action can be just as easily evaluated in terms of its end or result.

What some of these approaches to the problem of the 'near and dear' have in common is that they, in effect, treat special obligations or duties as fictions, albeit useful ones. Strictly speaking, one's relatives have no more moral standing than anyone else does. But it is useful for us to think and act *as* if they do have greater standing in many situations. The usefulness is derived from considerations such as those appealed to by Jackson in the sector argument. Thinking one's relatives are actually more deserving of your concern than strangers helps to generate focus on the well-being of those in one's circle, and this, given the epistemic and physical limitations we are all subject to, makes conduct, in general, more productive of the good.

Another option is to deny that value is exclusively neutral. One can keep the commitment to maximization of value and yet give up the view that value is purely neutral.[15] Perhaps some value is relative. Perhaps it is more good for me to give my attention to a family member than to a stranger. That is, it doesn't just *seem* more good to me, and it isn't simply that its seeming more good to me serves to promote neutral value more effectively. On this alternative, it is more good for me to pay more attention to those who are near and dear even when I realize that more neutral good could be achieved by my doing something else. It is better for Linda to give her daughter Monica a present of money rather than use that money to feed ten children via a gift to Oxfam (assuming, of course, that the money would make Monica happy). Linda is producing a better outcome *relative to Linda* by doing this. If Robert, who doesn't know Monica, gives money to Monica rather than the ten hungry children, this is not the case. It is better for Robert to give the money to the ten hungry children than to Monica. The explanation, again, is that this recognizes a category of agent-relative value, or good relative to an individual. If one develops consequentialism along these lines then the standard would be that the agent ought to maximize the good, or do what has the best consequences, *relative to her*. Linda should give the money to Monica, and Robert should not.

However, there are serious problems with this latter route. Agent-relative value is often cited in arguing for constraints (as well as permissions). Thus, it seems wrong for someone to kill one person even to prevent another person from killing two people. The idea is that for any given agent it is worse for that agent to kill one than to prevent two others from being killed. Killing one is the worse outcome for that agent. It is not the worse outcome impartially considered. But, if one does think that it is worse for an agent to kill one even to prevent two others from being killed by someone else, then one seemingly is committed to agent-relative value to provide a justification for this sort of constraint on our actions: we ought not to kill even to save others from being killed. But some have pointed out that this notion of agent-relative value doesn't stand up to careful scrutiny. After all, isn't it worse for *me* to kill one person now in order to prevent *myself* from killing two others in the future? If that intuition seems persuasive then we need to relativize value not simply to persons but to *times* at which persons have the option to act.[16]

Because appeals to agent-relative value seem rather ad hoc, and because the notion is itself problematic, most consequentialists still maintain that value is neutral.[17] We can justify acting as though there were agent-relative values, but the reasons appealed to reference agent-neutral value in the end.

The concern with equality is more difficult to accommodate. There is always the ad hoc maneuver of just holding equality itself to be an intrinsic good – and include it as an irreducible element of the value to be maximized in action. But more in keeping with the spirit of consequentialism is to hold that treating people equally is important because if we don't, more people are unhappy and unfulfilled. This strategy appeals to certain features of human nature, again. Scientists have noted that humans are extremely sensitive to their perceptions of unfairness and inequality. There is a good deal of evidence that we evolved to be able to pick out 'cheaters' and to deeply resent them, for example.[18] If someone is perceived to be receiving undeserved unequal shares, this is deeply resented. Resentment is a negative emotion. People don't enjoy feeling resentment. It doesn't make their lives go better, except, in some circumstances, as a means to achieve their desired end. So, people really care about equality. And, if people really care about it, it is important to their happiness. But critics would argue that this strategy doesn't fit well with how we feel about cheaters. We resent them because they did something bad; it's not the resentment itself that is bad because it is a 'negative' emotion. Instead the consequentialist is better off holding that we resent cheaters, justifiably, because they undermine productivity and incentives. Fairness in distribution is important because unfairness undermines motivation to be productive, to do one's job, to act well. And this undermines efforts at achieving overall happiness.

In the case of aggregation, total happiness is best. Later in the book I will be arguing that the standard involves total *actual* best consequences. There are numerous reasons for developing this line in spelling out the theory. Here, however, we merely need to observe the following: the standard for right action is that it produce the most total good effects. It does not follow that this specifies the correct decision-procedure for action. This is because the significance of the decision-procedure is instrumental to the outcome, and it is the outcome that really determines the action's moral quality. It is therefore a separate, and an empirical, issue as to what decision-procedure should be followed. But it seems very likely that improving the lives of already existing people is a very good bet, and doing so evenly insures against disastrous utility losses.

There is a problem with this approach that I call the 'gloomy pessimist' objection. Suppose that Mary has a certain amount of a benefit to hand out to others – money, let's say, since that can easily be translated into goods that satisfy preferences. Her options are to give it all to Sheila or all to Gloria, or equally divide it between the two. We are also assuming that neither is more 'deserving' than the other. Sheila is a happy-go-lucky person, sunny, cheerful, and would be incredibly delighted with the money, using it to take an art class she always wanted to take. Gloria, who has been sadly misnamed, is the sort of person who gets little pleasure from life. She sits at home, mostly, watching news and reality television shows, and complaining about the state of humanity. She would use the money to buy more cable access, so that she could have access to as much depressing news as possible. Should Mary give her some of the money, even though the money would make Sheila far more happy? On this view, maybe she should give Gloria half the money — given there's some value in an overall egalitarian decision-procedure. But it would not be the right thing to do if Gloria's recalcitrance is something that Mary is in a position to foresee. To some, this is counterintuitive, since both Sheila and Gloria deserve equal shares even if both don't derive equal levels of happiness. To argue otherwise, they would claim, gives rise to a utility monster objection.

The 'utility monster' is a creature thought up by Robert Nozick to illustrate that utilitarianism is not at all egalitarian, just because it holds that all persons' happiness counts equally. That's because one can imagine that some persons are happier than others given the same amount of resources as others. The extreme example of this is the utility monster:

> Utilitarian theory is embarrassed by the possibility of utility monsters who get enormously greater gains in utility from any sacrifice of others than these others lose. For, unacceptably, the theory seems to require that we all be sacrificed in the monster's maw, in order to increase total utility.[19]

The utility monster is a potential problem for the total utility view. The monster is the other extreme from the repugnant conclusion outcome. Here we have a single enormously happy (or fulfilled) being, whose happiness is at the expense of others, though others who would have been less happy than it with the same resources. One solution to these problems is to opt for improving welfare of already existing persons equally. But there can be a principled basis for this. For example, while it is true that given limited resources the right thing to do in distribution seems to be to distribute on the basis of who appreciates the resource most — diminishing marginal utility — but then the utility monster becomes a possibility, and that seems to violate our views of fairness. But we might think that in practice we need to make sure people reach a basic level of well-being before we do this. Further, it seems very plausible that it would de facto be unfair to distribute this way unless we could be sure that one person's welfare is really enhanced relative to others. Given a plausible view of human nature if we started distributing well-being on the basis of claims of enhanced welfare, we would end up with something very bad – so the best strategy just is the egalitarian one, but not because it is somehow intrinsically the best. It is the best in actual practice.

Our intuitions in these cases are influenced by views on entitlement, and what the real-life equivalent of utility monsters *ought* to want; what ought to make them happy. Monopolizing resources, even ones they really, really want, at the expense of others, seems immoral. But the only way to accommodate this seems to allow for what Rawls termed the 'separateness of persons' – people as individuals are owed consideration in themselves, not simply as member of a collective happiness, or welfare, pool.

Derek Parfit notes that the utility monster scenario is just difficult to get a grip on, since for such a monster to exist it would have to be vastly different from anything in our experience – a Godlike being. He asks us to imagine the world's population living in truly wretched circumstances while the vast bulk of resources go to Nozick's monster, who we must imagine has an awesomely vast quality of life, a quality of life

> *millions* of times as high as that of anyone we know. Can we imagine this? Think of the life of the luckiest person that you know, and ask what a life would have to be like in order to be a million times as much worth living. The qualitative gap between such a life and ours, at its best, must resemble the gap between ours, at its best, and the life of those creatures who are barely conscious – such as, if they *are* conscious, Plato's "contented oysters". It seems a fair reply that we cannot imagine, even in the dimmest way, the life of this Utility Monster.[20]

But he also notes that the scenario still puts pressure on act-utilitarianism.[21] He changes it so that the force of the example can be felt without having to imagine a being such as the one described above. It is the repugnant conclusion that gets the greater total utility by increasing the number of persons, not increasing the level of utility experienced by a single person. This does get one out of the conceivability problem. However, it doesn't serve the same purpose. It doesn't raise the 'fairness' flag in the same way as Nozick's case.

One way to approach the equality problem with total aggregation is to argue that there are two distinct parameters along which we need to aggregate: we need to consider the least well-off separately, and prioritize their well-being over the well-being of others in the group that we are considering.[22] This general line of thought is often referred to as 'prioritarianism'. It would be a mistake to simply argue that equality itself is to be aimed for separately, since this would lead to condoning the 'leveling-down' of well-being – taking away benefits from the well-off simply to bring them in line with the less well-off, and that seems quite unjust. Instead, one can hold that taking some benefits from the most well-off is justified on equality grounds, but only if it benefits the least well-off. Further additions to existing well-being of the most well-off would only be justified if they also promoted the well-being of the least well-off. The fundamental idea is that in aggregating preference, additional weight be given to the well-being of the least well-off.

One issue with prioritarianism is the following: suppose that in the group we are considering, Ralph is the least well-off. He lives in a box on the street and eats only when strangers take pity on him and buy him some food. However, Ralph is largely responsible for his lack of well-being. He was raised in a prosperous and nurturing home, attended an excellent college, and is capable of holding a job. He just doesn't want to because he values the freedom of not being tied down in any way. Some might argue that it would be wrong to weight Ralph's well-being more heavily than others. Thus, a very simple form of prioritarianism would seem to give us the wrong answer here – if we judge people responsible for their lack of well-being, it doesn't seem fair or right to give their well-being preference or more weight in aggregation.

However, prioritarians have responded to these concerns with more sophisticated versions of their theory. For example, Richard Arneson develops a prioritarian approach to considerations of justice in distribution that he terms "responsibility-catering prioritarianism." This is the view that "justice requires us to maximize a function of human well-being that gives priority to improving the well-being of those who are badly off and of those who, if badly off, are not substantially responsible for their condition."[23] This is combined with a luck egalitarian view in which it is deemed unfair that some people suffer due to bad luck, due to factors completely beyond their control. Consider Ronald, who, unlike Ralph, has been born into poverty and has been raised in an abusive environment. Ronald works very hard to improve his life, but because he got such a bad start he has had a very difficult time finding a decent job. Ronald's problems are not the result of anything that he did. They are the result of bad luck. On Arneson's view, it is the well-being of people like Ronald, not Ralph, that is to be given priority.

Note that prioritarianism is still a form of consequentialism, it is just not standard utilitarianism since it rejects strict impartiality. Prioritarianism is a variation on consequentialism that seems intuitively very plausible. In favoring a leveling-up strategy for promoting the well-being of the least well-off in society, it is in keeping with the benevolent motivations behind the development of utilitarianism. Nevertheless, implementing it raises a number of difficult issues. For example, *how much* extra weight does one give to the least well-off members of the group? Does one give them double weight? Triple? How does one non-arbitrarily decide on a cutoff between least well-off and the rest of the group? The bottom 5, 10, or 20 percent?

Prioritarians would approach these questions as worries having to do with implementing the approach. For example, one could adopt a sliding scale along which one weights different groups differently depending on where they fall on the scale – the lower 5 percent being weighted more heavily than the next 5 percent, and so on.

So far the discussion has focused on how we determine what is, overall, the best state of affairs. The approach to this up to now has been to aggregate over particular 'good for' judgments, judgments that something is good for an individual, and then add up those goods, subtract the corresponding bads, to get the overall result. Prioritarianism introduces a variation on the simple approach, but it is still a fairly intuitive approach to aggregation.

Another important issue – which introduces another complication – has to do with how to go about aggregating the well-being of *future* persons. Does the happiness of future persons count or not? Here's the dilemma. The consequentialist holds that one ought to maximize the good. Does this mean, for example, that people ought to try to have as many children as possible, as long as they can be reasonably certain that those children will live overall happy lives – that is, lives that are overall worth living? This places an extraordinary reproductive burden on people, and is a rather extreme illustration of the general demandingness problem. Some consequentialists argue that the injunction to maximize the good is restricted to those persons who already exist, that is, to *actual* persons rather than future persons. This would solve the above problem, but leads to other puzzles. So most of us believe that we have obligations to future persons, persons who will be living, let's say, 200 years from now and who we believe have some claim to clean water and lovely forests. We do think it intuitively plausible to count their happiness when it comes to deciding what we ought to do. Should we drill for oil in a certain location? Well, it may help in the short term, but will then leave people in the future without that resource. And what it means for people in the future is taken to be one relevant consideration in our deliberations. Ignoring their happiness and well-being, even though they don't yet exist, seems irresponsible. So the strategy of claiming that only actual persons count seems problematic for this reason.

One thing we could try is to make finer metaphysical distinctions and see how those track our moral intuitions. So far we have talked about actual persons and non-existent persons. The person actualists tend to argue that it is really weird to hold the view that non-existent persons have rights or entitlements. For one thing, one cannot make a promise to someone who doesn't exist. In order for A to make a promise to B, B needs to understand that A has made a commitment – this is called the 'uptake' condition on promising. In the case of future persons, there is no one to satisfy the 'uptake' condition. Since we can't incur obligations to non-existent persons through promising, this casts doubt on obligations to the non-existent in general. But this seems to be highly counterintuitive. For one thing, we do seem to have some obligations with respect to infants and animals, even though such beings lack the cognitive architecture necessary for 'uptake'. Further, while many people disagree about the nature of obligations to future generations, almost everyone thinks that there are things we could do now that would be unfair with respect to future generations – such as using up all the natural resources. And in some respects consequentialism can give you a really good answer here – we need to count their well-being because it is a part of overall well-being. But then we get back to the birth-control problem. Of course, there are many people who hold that we ought to have as many children as possible, so they would happily bite this bullet. Indeed, they would not even see it as a bullet. But assuming we disagree, there is an issue here to be sorted out. The difference between simple non-existing people and the people who do have a claim on us and who as of yet don't exist is that they will actually exist, though they do not actually exist now. They are non-existent at t_1 but existent at t_2, where t_2 is a future time. These people are not identifiable in the way that actual persons are. But it is a mistake to view them, really, as not actual. They are actual future people, but not actual present people. The contrast is with persons who will not exist at a future time. These persons are possible, but only that. At any given time in the present we will not be able to identify the actual future persons and distinguish them as individuals, nor distinguish them from other possible future persons. But identifiability is not a condition of moral considerability. Consider the following: Melissa desperately wants to have a baby, and has arranged for the doctor to implant her with five embryos at some future date, thinking that only one will survive. Indeed, the doctor tells her that only one will survive to full term. Melissa decides that she needs to refrain from consuming alcohol and taking drugs before becoming pregnant, because the baby that will be born benefits from this. The individual who will be born is not yet identifiable by her, yet it still seems that she certainly ought to consider the future individual's welfare in her calculations – the future individual she has extremely good evidence will actually come into existence. Other common-sense cases help to illustrate the point. Most people are in favor of seat-belt laws because, when the number-crunching is done at the end of the year, it can be shown that many more people are alive who otherwise would not be. However, it is extremely difficult to identify who in particular is saved through the use of a seat belt, since the act of wearing a seat belt itself might influence what accidents occur – if timing is a factor in at least some car accidents, as seems likely. But the law is justified because it produces a better state of affairs, overall, even if it is not possible to identify particular persons for whom the law has proven beneficial.

Chapter summary

This chapter is about the issue of aggregation of utility. Should we maximize total good or the average amount of good? Each approach has difficulties, which are discussed in the chapter, as well as problems involving whose well-being should be included in the aggregation. This raises the important issue of future generations. Future people do not yet exist. Should we consider the effects our actions will have on future people in considering what our moral obligations are? If so, then we need to include the well-being of even non-existent persons in our moral deliberations.

Further reading

An all-time classic is Derek Parfit, *Reasons and Persons* (Oxford University Press, 1984), where numerous problems revolving around the issue of aggregation are discussed.

John Broome, *Weighing Goods* (New York: Oxford University Press, 1991); *Weighing Lives* (New York: Oxford University Press, 2004).

Tim Mulgan, *Future People* (New York: Oxford University Press, 2006).

Gustaf Arrhenius, Jesper Ryberg, and Torbjörn Tännsjö, "The Repugnant Conclusion," in *The Stanford Encyclopedia of Philosophy* (Fall 2008 ed.), ed. E. Zalta. Online. Available HTTP: <http://plato.stanford.edu/archives/fall2008/entries/repugnant-conclusion/>.

4

INDIRECTION

In the last chapter we discussed standard problems with utilitarianism understood as the view that the right action is the action, among those which are open to the agent, or genuine alternatives for the agent, that maximizes the good. This formulation is termed 'act-consequentialism' and is a form of *direct* consequentialism since one determines the moral status of the action on the basis of what the action *itself*, that is, 'directly', produces in terms of good effects.

One significant problem with the direct, act-consequentialist approach has to do with the seeming incompatibility with both distributive justice and retributive justice. In the case outlined earlier in the book, we imagined a sheriff confronted with the choice between allowing an innocent person to be killed by a mob, or allowing twenty innocent children to be trampled to death by the same mob. He should not allow the man to be hanged by the mob – that violates our principles of justice. Yet, the act-utilitarian seems to be committed to holding that allowing the innocent man to be hanged is the right thing to do because it leads to the death of only one innocent person, as opposed to twenty. I mentioned a few ways for the act-utilitarian to try to avoid this conclusion, or to embrace it in a way that didn't seem so counterintuitive. But there is another option for the utilitarian here. That is to pursue what I term the *indirection strategy*. An indirect utilitarian holds that the right *action* is the action performed in accordance with (or as a result of), *something else* that maximizes the good, such as a set of rules, or a type of motivation.

(IS) Define 'right action' in terms of consequences generated by some other entity the action is related to (either causally or conceptually).

Perhaps the most prominent form of indirect consequentialism is rule-utilitarianism.

The rule-utilitarian holds that the right action is not the action that results in the best overall consequences, rather it is the action performed in accordance with the set of rules which maximize the good. On the simple case we considered, then, one could hold that one rule in our set of rules is something like 'Don't hand over an innocent person to a mob'. Thus, the right action would be the refusal to hand over the innocent person to the mob. This is still consequentialism, however, because the rules themselves are justified solely on the basis of promoting the good.

The above characterization is very vague and needs a good deal of unpacking. For example, one could hold that the right action is the action performed in accordance with the set of rules that would be best under actual circumstances, ideal circumstances, or some hybrid – such as the set of rules that would be best if actual people were to internalize them consistently.

Why not simply hold that the right action is the action that is performed in accordance with a set of rules that promotes utility, under the circumstances in which the action is performed? One reason against this formulation is that actual circumstances in which an action is performed can be, morally speaking, rather grim. This can lead to skewed results regarding what counts as the right action. Suppose, for example, that 500 years ago beating one's wife was considered obligatory under certain circumstances, such that if a husband failed to beat his wife under those circumstances he himself would be imprisoned and his wife beaten in any case. Now, in actual circumstances such as these, following the rule 'Beat one's wife (under conditions C)' might maximize the good – but only because social norms are such that punishments have been set up to hurt those who do not live up to that particular rule. Even so, beating one's wife is wrong. However, if the right action is defined in terms of a set of rules the following of which *maximizes* the good, this can be avoided, since the best set of rules would not include either the wife-beating rule or the punishment rule. Even so, a critic would note that if we are contextualizing the set of rules to what would maximize the good given what actual people at a given time believe and desire, we could still get results that are intuitively incorrect.

Suppose the rules are flexible enough that one isn't presented with the problems that standardly afflict absolutist systems. So, for example, one wouldn't want a rule as rigid as 'Don't break a promise no matter what'; rather, the rule should recognize that there are circumstances, maybe very extreme circumstances, in which it is permissible, or even obligatory, to break a promise, such as 'to save a person's life'. That's because some exceptions to simple rules maximize the good. However, if one goes this way, in which rules are specified in enough detail to avoid implausible absolutism that results in intentionally failing to maximize the good, then the criticism is that it is de facto the same as act-consequentialism. That is, it may be *intensionally* distinct in that it formally defines 'right action' differently from act-consequentialism, but it is *extensionally* equivalent in that it picks out the same set of actions as 'right' and the same set of actions as 'wrong'.[1] So, for all practical purposes, it is the same. If this is so, then the theory loses much of the motivation behind it, which was to show how it, rather than act-consequentialism, advocates sticking to rules in the face of failures to promote the good.

A contemporary rule-consequentialist approach is developed by Brad Hooker.

> An act is wrong if and only if it is forbidden by the code of rules whose internalization by the overwhelming majority of everyone everywhere in each new generation has maximum expected value in terms of well-being (with some priority for the worst off). The calculation of a code's expected value includes all costs of getting the code internalized. If in terms of expected value two or more codes are better than the rest but equal to one another, the one closest to conventional morality determines what acts are wrong.[2]

This is also supposed to take into consideration the cognitive and affective limitations of the persons internalizing the code, and requires rules "whose publicity would have good consequences" and "whose internalization would be cost-effective."[3] The account of well-being that Hooker favors is a version of the objective list theory.

Hooker argues that his approach avoids the problems of earlier approaches. First, it doesn't just collapse into act-consequentialism, because Hooker holds that the right system of rules must be internalized and the principle 'Maximize the good', if internalized, would lead to disaster:

> [I]f we had just the one rule 'Maximize the good', sooner or later awareness of this would become widespread. And becoming aware of this would undermine people's ability to rely confidently on others to behave in agreed

upon ways. Trust would break down. In short, terrible consequences would
result from the public expectation that this rule would prescribe killing,
stealing, and so on when such acts would maximize the good.[4]

This argument strikes me as odd. We should keep distinct the issue of truth
from the issue of usefulness, and this argument seems to conflate them. It
may well be that it is true that we ought to maximize the good and that the
best way to do this is to follow rules that are so internalized and enforced
that people can rely on and trust each other to do the right thing. But this,
by itself, is nothing an act-utilitarian would disagree with at all. Indeed, act-
consequentialists hold that rules of thumb can be very useful. It's just that
they are overridable. And this leads to the other horn of the dilemma for
Hooker. Are the rules overridable? He argues that we needn't have strict and
rigid adherence to rules, since in his ideal system there will be a 'prevent
disaster' clause. So, while it is true that I should keep my promise even if
failure to do so would result in marginal utility gains, it is permissible or
even obligatory for me to break my promise in order to save someone's life
(given that the loss of a life qualifies as a 'disaster' on his view). But this
'prevent disaster' is a point of vulnerability for his theory. It shows he does
believe that rules are overridable. It cuts against the indirection, really. One
could get the same results with the standard act-consequentialist approach
that takes into consideration things like our fallibilities and epistemic limitations. The act-consequentialist is not against the use of rules, after all. Rules
are perfectly good – they promote efficiency in decision-making, which is
an important consideration. It's just that rules for the act-consequentialist
function as 'rules of thumb' providing guides for actions, but ones that can
be overridden in cases where there is a clear and truly overall utility gain.
The act-consequentialist could even hold that the presumption should be in
favor of the rule – given our experience, the rule in question is accepted as
a good rule of thumb precisely because it captures the sorts of utility judgments made in the past – so that we need to be very careful and cautious in
overriding one of these rules and proceed only when the gain is clear. Thus,
in building in the 'prevent disaster' clause Hooker avoids the problem of
absolutism, but then loses a significant motive for developing rule-consequentialism as an alternative to act-consequentialism.

    The overall problem with the approach, and the major reason it lacks
currency amongst most contemporary consequentialists, is that it presents
the theorist with seriously unpalatable theoretical choices. Either one
accepts the rigidity of the rules and gets stuck with absolutism, and worse, a

decision situation which seems to call for irrationality – which seems to call for intentionally going against the overall good – or one accepts flexibility, and then loses the primary motivation for taking the indirect approach in the first place. Allowing that the rules be complicated and incorporating exceptions, so as to avoid the first horn of the dilemma, leads to a de facto act-consequentialism. David Lyons made this point using the intensional/ extensional equivalence distinction. Consider the two different kinds of definitions, (AC) and (RC):

> (AC) An act is right iff it produces the most good.
> (RC) An act is right iff it is performed in accordance with a system of rules that produces the most good.

(AC) and (RC) are not intensionally equivalent, since they define 'right action' differently. However, Lyons notes, they may pick out the very same class of actions, and thus be extensionally equivalent, if we interpret (RC) flexibly – to allow for complicated rules that take account of contexts, for example, in which lying might promote the good. And, if this is the case, there is no practical distinction between the two. Keeping the practical distinction in place allows it to solve a problem, but then makes it wildly implausible in other ways. If there is no practical distinction, then why opt for (RC) in the first place? Again, Brad Hooker argues that his version avoids this dilemma. The 'no disaster' clause allows him to keep simple rules, just adding that clause. But this makes the theory very underdescribed, and one wonders in filling in details as to what counts as a disaster – how bad things have to get, and so forth – will we again end up with something *de facto* the same as (AC)? Or just irrational?

Another line of attack often used against the rule-consequentialist is to argue that it doesn't get reasons for actions quite right. On the rule-consequentialist view, the right thing to do, for example, is to keep your promises even in cases where breaking the promise generates a better outcome. The point of opting for this indirect approach to evaluation is to allow for something that looks like a deontic constraint but is ultimately justified by consequentialist reasons. But if Mary decides to keep her promise, and if she justifies it indirectly, as the rule-consequentialist seems to hold, then the justification looks odd. In effect, the criticism goes, Mary is using, as a reason to keep her promise, the consideration that, in general, keeping promises maximizes the good, or is part of a system of norms which, in general, maximize the good. And this simply doesn't capture how the normal person justifies these actions.[5] According to this line of attack, the appropriate justification for keeping one's promise is just *that one promised*, period. It isn't something like, if people in general keep promises good will be maximized. This resembles the schizophrenia objection leveled against consequentialism more generally. On the one hand, one keeps a promise simply because one has made it – that is one's motive. On the other hand, what justifies the action is something else – the fact that keeping the promise generates more good effects. The complaint is that there is a disconnect between the agent's motives and her justifications which serves to 'alienate' her from morality.

My view is that this doesn't really represent a serious problem for the rule-consequentialist (or any consequentialist), for several reasons. One is that it does make sense to hold that one can go beyond 'well, I promised' in giving reasons for keeping the promise. And it makes sense to appeal to rules in doing this – by holding that we need to stick to rules that promote the good, for example. The real problem here is to keep the view distinct from act-consequentialism, which also holds that rules, albeit rules of thumb, are good justifications.

Further, this line of attack is often presented as a problem for indirection. But the intuition that drives it isn't generalizable to other forms of indirect consequentialism. One we will discuss below, virtue-consequentialism, for example, has the agent appealing to virtue as the justification for keeping promises. This accords quite well with our intuitions that would hold that in blameworthy promise-breaking cases there is some lack of virtue being demonstrated by the agent.

1.1 Motive-consequentialism: direct and indirect

Robert Adams introduced another version of indirect consequentialism with motive-utilitarianism. On this view the moral quality of the action will depend upon the consequences generated by the *motive* behind the action. If the motive is such that acting on that motive generally produces good effects, then the action performed on the basis of that motive is the right action. On Adams' view the best sort of person is characterized on this view as the person who has the most useful, or utility-producing, sets of motivations that he or she can have. What makes a motivational set a good one is that it is the set that has a tendency to good production, even if, in my particular circumstances, it does not produce the good.

Motive-consequentialism need not be spelled out as an indirect theory. One could have a view that the primary focus of evaluation is motive rather than action, and then argue that the 'right' motive is the one such that it produces the best effects. This could be done via action, but perhaps not. For example, one could argue that the right motive for someone to act on has other benefits, such as positive internal states like pleasure. These internal states are not caused by the motive, though they depend on the motive. For example, when John thinks about attending his ex-wife's wedding, the best motive for him to have, and thus the right motive, is to be good – to be motivated by a sense of dignity and generosity, rather than jealousy. This will generate good behavior, but such a motive is also indicative of good internal psychological states such as a feeling of self-respect. This need not be caused by the motive itself, indeed, it could in some way be part of what causes the agent to be motivated appropriately. But there is a dependence of one form or another, and this is part of what makes the motive good in consequentialist terms. However, if one believes that the focus of evaluation is action, and that the point of morality is to guide action, then one would opt for the indirect version of motive-consequentialism.

One could also develop a kind of virtue-consequentialism that holds that the right action is the action performed from a disposition that is a virtue disposition (i.e. is such that it produces more good than not, for example). On this view, one gives a consequentialist account of what makes a given disposition a virtue, and then defines right action as 'the action the person with the virtue would perform under the circumstances'. This form of consequentialism seems to have the advantage of being able to accommodate the justice case, since justice is a virtue and handing over an innocent man to a mob is surely unjust. It can also, in a very natural way, handle other problems that had been brought up for straightforward act-consequentialism. One, in particular, is the problem of how to incorporate a consideration of special relationships – such as family relationships and friendships – into one's moral theory. Utilitarianism, given that it seems to require that agents try to maximize the good, would seem to require a motivational set that is, some argue, incompatible with these special relationships. On virtue-consequentialism, it may be right for a mother to favor her children, since such favor is considered a motherly virtue – the world is a better place when mothers favor their children (within certain reasonable parameters). The key would be to show that relationship-favoring dispositions are ones which do produce good on balance, and then hold that, since we understand 'right' in terms of actions that these dispositions favor, there is, in fact, no incompatibility between virtue-consequentialism and our intuitions about special obligations and permissions with respect to friends and relatives.

This alternative suggests a view of 'right action' at odds with standard act-consequentialism. This is because there may be more than one good disposition, or virtue, relevant to a given issue. Thus, there may be more than one right action with respect to that issue. This form of indirection would avoid a criticism often made against consequentialism – that it unrealistically holds that there is only one right action with respect to a given choice situation. This criticism was leveled most prominently by Rosalind Hursthouse, who believed that moral decision-making was a very messy sort of enterprise.[6] There are often cases where there is no single determinate right answer, on her view. Indeed, consider the example of someone who is contemplating having an abortion. On Hursthouse's view whether it is right or wrong will depend on whether her motivation is virtuous, or, rather, characteristic of virtue. If she decides to have the abortion because she has five other young children to care for and would be overwhelmed by the pregnancy and new baby, then perhaps it is the right thing to do. If she decides to have the abortion because it would anger her husband, then it is the wrong thing to do. There's no one right or wrong answer. Thus, moral reality is messy, and on Hursthouse's view the consequentialist seems to overlook this by demanding a false sort of precision to 'rightness'.

Of course, we need to distinguish different sorts of messiness. The consequentialist is not claiming that agents always know the single right action; we are epistemically very limited beings – not only about empirical facts, but also when it comes to the truth or falsity (or appropriateness or inappropriateness) of our normative values and commitments. Thus, at most the consequentialist is committed to a kind of metaphysical tidiness about morality; but the epistemology is an entirely different matter.[7]

Virtue-consequentialism, at least in the simple form presented here, suffers from a failure to guide action in a determinate way. Even those, such as Hursthouse, who hold that there is no legitimate determinacy, should be worried that so little concrete guidance is provided. There are ways to solve the problem, ways that would require further exploration. For example, one could rank virtues in consequentialist terms, and hold that the right action is the action performed from the best relevant virtue for the situation in question, that is, the virtue that tends to produce more good than the alternative. For example, suppose that beneficence towards the needy produces better results than respect for desert; the right action, then, might be to tax the wealthy to help the needy even though one is taxing them against their will. It would just involve another consequentialist trade-off, at the level of virtue, among those virtues applicable in the situation at hand.

Indirect forms of consequentialism *all* suffer from the problem that they tend to recommend irrational courses of action. The cases that motivate the approach, where indirection seems intuitively plausible, trade on the underdescription of cases. Or, as in the case of virtue-consequentialism, no clear guidance on what to do is provided, since widely variant courses of action are compatible with different moral virtues. A good mother may favor her children over others, but a good judge does not. In awarding government jobs, the right thing to do is to give it to the most deserving, rather than one's own child, even if we think that good *parents* favor their own children. The virtuous parent may not do the morally right thing. If we fail to preserve this distinction we fail to preserve something really valuable in our evaluative practices. Indeed, of some acts it seems quite natural to say things like "She acted as a good mother would, but she still did something wrong." The virtue-consequentialist could respond by noting that, first and foremost, the virtuous parent must be a virtuous human being – but then this does not allow us to solve the problems that pushed our intuitions towards adopting virtue-consequentialism. The virtuous human being does not favor his children over the children of others when it comes to distribution of public goods, because such favoritism would be wrong. And it would be wrong because those particular actions tend to lead to bad effects.

But it is important to point out that the direct approach can have a place for virtue evaluation, motive evaluation, and so forth. These things are all subject to consequentialist evaluation, just as actions are. This direct approach to moral evaluation is *global consequentialism* in its most general form. I will be defending this approach in the remainder of the book.

Chapter summary

Some consequentialists think that difficulties with act-consequentialism make it too problematic. One serious problem is that act-consequentialism seems, in principle, anyway, incompatible with our intuitions about justice, since the theory might require that we actually violate someone's rights in order to promote overall good. Thus, some consequentialists opt for alternatives to direct act-consequentialism by using an indirection strategy that involves defining 'right action' not in terms of the consequences of the action itself, but in terms of the consequences of something else associated with the action. The most prominent version is rule-consequentialism, which very roughly holds that the right action is the action performed in accordance with a set of rules whose adoption maximizes the good. The strengths and weaknesses of this approach are discussed in this chapter.

Further reading

Brad Hooker, *Ideal Code, Real World* (Oxford: Oxford University Press, 2000).
Robert Adams, "Motive Utilitarianism," *Journal of Philosophy* 73 (1976), 467–81.
A classic on types of utilitarianism is David Lyons, *Forms and Limits of Utilitarianism* (Oxford: Clarendon Press, 1965).

5

OBJECTIVE AND SUBJECTIVE CONSEQUENTIALISM

Consequentialists disagree amongst themselves about whether it is the actual consequences produced by an action that matter morally, or the intended (or expected, or foreseen) consequences. Those who believe that it is the actual consequences, independent of the agent's psychological states, which determine moral quality are objective consequentialists. Those who hold that it is the intended or foreseen consequences are subjective consequentialists, since they tie the moral quality to the agent's psychology – what the agent believes and/or desires. Earlier in the book, when the demandingness problem was discussed, the distinction was introduced to show how consequentialists could accommodate intuitions about why we give preference to the 'near and dear'. In this chapter a more detailed argument will be provided for the objective version of the theory.

Objective consequentialism (OC) appeals to a basic insight. What actually happens in the world as a result of someone's action matters morally, and this is separate from features of the agent's actual psychology.[1] G. E. Moore gave voice to this insight when he set out the standard in *Principia Ethica*:

> [T]o assert that a certain line of conduct is, at a given time, absolutely right or obligatory, is obviously to assert that more good or less evil will exist in the world, if it be adopted than if anything else be done instead.[2]

Moore might have been somewhat optimistic in declaring this "obviously" the case. However, there is a good deal of evidence that this standard reflects our considered views regarding moral significance. For example, Richard Brandt made a case for the objective standard by discussing the following scenario:

> Consider Eisenhower's position at the summit conference in 1960. Khrushchev demanded that Eisenhower apologize, as a condition for negotiation. Let us suppose that Eisenhower proceeded to ask himself the moral question, "What is the morally right thing for me to do now? Is it my moral obligation to apologize or to refuse to apologize?" ... [I]f he did try to answer this question, he must have considered many things. ... Let us suppose that Eisenhower surveyed these points as carefully as possible with his advisors and came to a conclusion. ... [I]t was not his duty to apologize, that on the contrary it was his duty *not* to apologize.[3]

Brandt then notes that even after careful reflection on the pros and cons of apologizing Eisenhower's conclusion could be something along the lines of "*Probably* it is my duty not to apologize." This seems to indicate that even after careful reflection, to the full extent of his capacities and those of his advisors, he still isn't sure. Yet on the subjective view he ought to be sure that he is right. The measure of one's moral success on at least one very appealing version of the subjective view is the extent to which one acts in good faith on one's genuine expectation of optimal consequences.

Further, Eisenhower might later come to recognize that he had been mistaken in the moral conclusion, and that, indeed, he did have a duty to apologize, in spite of his careful reflection on the issue. Both of these observations lend strength to there at least being a significant sense in which we view 'right' objectively. Further, in the *actualism* literature a good deal of attention is paid to how one is to advise someone to act, based on what one knows about their future behavior. The advice should always track what you think is going to actually happen, not what you think the advisee believes will happen, or even what the advisee believes, with justification, will happen.[4]

That there is a useful objective sense of 'right' is generally not contested by subjective consequentialists. Their view is that even if there is a distinct sense of 'right' that is objective, this sense either is not 'primary' or it is itself derivative from the subjective standard of 'right'. The debate seems to center on which sort of right is 'primary' – if there is a primary sense at all. In defending objective consequentialism one defends it as the *standard* of 'right' that has *explanatory priority* with respect to the subjective standard. I do not think that this version of the objective standard is correct as a matter of definition, which would make the objective view analytic. This would render any who disagree incoherent, which seems like a rather unrealistically extreme mistake to attribute to them. Again, the correctness of the objective standard is owed to its *explanatory* primacy, which is understood, I believe, relative to its role in meta-evaluation. This is the claim that objectivists are pressing. This is not to say that the objective 'ought' is *deliberatively prior*. Indeed, the nature of the objective approach would make this claim hard to even spell out.

The explanatory priority of the objective standard accounts for why praise and blame are appropriate in certain types of moral deliberation. For example, if good intentions are good it is *because* they promote the good. It may even be the case that the subjective standard is deliberatively prior (in the sense that it sets the norm for how agents ought to be deliberating), but that the deliberative priority of the subjective standard is justified by the objective standard. Before outlining this view, however, we should consider why the subjective standard itself seems so compelling.

In the contemporary literature, the original formulation of the distinction was first made by Peter Railton:

> *Subjective consequentialism* is the view that whenever one faces a choice of actions, one should attempt to determine which act of those available would most promote the good, and should then try to act accordingly. ... *Objective consequentialism* is the view that the criterion of the rightness of an act or course of action is whether it in fact would most promote the good of those acts available to the agent.[5]

Railton was arguing in favor of objective consequentialism. As he explicitly notes above, it is the view that the *criterion* or standard of right "is whether in fact it would most promote the good." But the notion, on his view, is important because he is trying to defend someone who holds that such a criterion is the correct criterion from the charge that he cannot be a good friend, or favor the near and dear, and still be a good consequentialist. That is, he is trying to paint a sympathetic picture of someone who is *committed* to the standard as a standard of right. But it is important to note that the standard, as a *criterion* of right, operates independently of an agent's commitment to it: an action is right if and only if, on this view, it actually produces the most good, or the best outcome overall, regardless of what the agent was thinking at the time she performed the action. The above passage indicates that the question that concerned Railton had more to do with deciding between a standard, which is objective, and a decision-procedure, which is subjective. There was then a later slide to viewing the decision-procedure, in the case of the subjective consequentialist, as containing or referring to the standard itself. Thus, a subjective standard of right quite naturally seems to go with a decision-procedure, which, by its nature, is subjective.

Thus, there are two issues that need to be kept distinct: the issue of criterion, or standard, of right, and the issue of what the consequentialist decision-procedure is like. On the issue of standards, one can be an objective or a subjective consequentialist, holding in the first case that right depends upon actual good produced, or in the second case that it depends on something such as expected good. The decision-procedure issue is separate. One could hold an objective standard, and also hold that one ought to use a decision-procedure in which one tries to maximize expected good. Or one could hold a subjective standard, and also hold that the right decision-procedure appeals to the same content as the standard, such as 'try to try to promote the good'. Or one could be objective in terms of the standard, and leave open, as an empirical issue, what the correct decision-procedures are in promoting the good. The latter is Railton's approach. But his disagreement with the subjectivist is really focused on what the correct *standard* is.

Suppose that we have a standard, one that everyone basically agrees on, in which 1 foot is understood as '12 inches'. This standard could be given an objective and a subjective interpretation, 'what is actually 12 inches' or 'what the judger believes to be 12 inches'. Aside from the standards issue, there is also the issue of how to measure a foot properly. One might believe that the best test for whether one has actually measured a foot is to be guided by one's beliefs about length, and measurement, and so forth. A consequentialist can similarly be subjective in two different ways: either by adopting a subjective standard and a subjective decision-procedure, or by adopting the subjective decision-procedure, but keeping the objective standard. In the remainder of the chapter the sense of subjective discussed is the first – in which the standard of *right* is determined by what the agent expects to be brought about by her actions. One motivation for adopting the standard, however, has to do with the plausibility of the subjective decision-procedure. If one recommends a certain decision-procedure, then should that not itself contain the standard of right? This doesn't seem to follow in the moral case, however, any more than it does in the measurement case. The intuition that the agent's actual beliefs and expectations matter is explained by holding that the standard of *praiseworthiness* is subjective.

People committed to the objective standard are perfectly able to have good-producing dispositions, and they are acting well, even though not explicitly following a consequentialist decision-procedure in deciding what to do in all cases. Rather, the consequentialist standard of 'right' is *regulative* for them. It serves as a psychological touchstone, used for critical assessment of dispositions to act. Pro-relationship dispositions, such as those involved in forming friendships and close attachments, pass this review on Railton's view since these are necessary for the normal human being to live a good life. The positive side of the consequentialist's empirical sensitivity is that the theory takes seriously, in practice, facts of human psychology. One fact about human beings is that they are social creatures who live in communities with other human beings, and who treasure and value relationships with others.

Railton suggests that the standard is a regulative ideal since he is primarily concerned with defending consequentialism from the 'alienation' objection that holds that a consequentialist practical deliberator is committed to renouncing personal commitments and feelings in order to grind out actions that are simply calculated to maximize overall good. In contrast to this bleak vision of consequentialist practical reason, Railton's 'sophisticated' consequentialists avoid alienation from the values that justify their actions by holding the consequentialist criterion of 'right' as a regulative ideal. Thus, the sophisticated consequentialist employs the criterion, but not all the time. Instead, she cultivates dispositions to act that are themselves good-promoting dispositions, though, again, she will occasionally use the consequentialist criterion to critically review her dispositions and behavior.

The alienation criticism was put forward, in various guises, by writers such as Bernard Williams and Michael Stocker, and then pursued by other writers arguing that consequentialism was incompatible with friendship and other personal relationships that, by their very nature, are partial rather than impartial.[6] The challenge, however, is effectively met by objective consequentialism. A good friend is not one who constantly engages in consequentialist evaluations of her relationships. Yet – as Railton sees it – neither is she one who utterly avoids critical assessment of relationships. In the case of the sophisticated consequentialist, that critical assessment is relative to an objective standard. In reflective moments the standard can be appealed to, she can take stock and assess her actions and character relative to this standard. There is an assumption that a commitment to the standard (which is distinct from the standard itself) in some form actually does help produce better overall consequences.

Some writers have argued that Railton's view of how a sophisticated consequentialist operates is actually incompatible with the very relationships he views as good for human beings to participate in. If that is the case, it does not impact on the standard itself. One could then argue, as an objective consequentialist, that this would simply demonstrate that Railton happens to be wrong about what really does produce the best state of affairs. The issue of the correct standard is separable from the issue of the correct mode of practical deliberation needed to fulfill the standard.

Railton was not the first to note that there is a crucial difference between standard and decision-procedure. The view that consequentialism sets a standard *rather than* establishes the moral requirement of a consequentialist motive was first articulated by Sidgwick, who argued that:

> [T]he doctrine that Universal Happiness is the ultimate *standard* must not be understood to imply that Universal Benevolence is the only right or always best *motive* of action. For ... it is not necessary that the end which gives the criterion of rightness should always be the end at which we consciously aim: and if experience shows that the general happiness will be more satisfactorily attained if men frequently act from other motives than pure universal philanthropy, it is obvious that these other motives are reasonably to be preferred on Utilitarian principles.[7]

Of course, Sidgwick distinguished motive from intention, and the same observations don't necessarily hold for intention, but Sidgwick recognized the fundamental distinction between the content of the agent's psychology and the standard we used to evaluate the agent's actions, character traits, and so forth. The same observation was picked up on by Eugene Bales, who held that a good deal of the criticism of utilitarianism rested on conflating the two.[8] Bales also uses this to show that rule-utilitarian criticisms of act-utilitarianism are unfounded (see Chapter 3). Derek Parfit, too, noted the distinction in arguing that consequentialism is potentially self-effacing (given some plausible empirical claims).

Another worry about the objective standard is that it is not practical. Railton, for example, notes that some argue that such a standard is not action-guiding. He rebuts this worry by noting that:

> [O]bjective consequentialism sets a definite and distinctive criterion of right action, and it becomes an empirical question (though not an easy one) which modes of decision making should be employed and when.[9]

In fact, Frank Jackson argues that this is a major weakness of Railton's account. As he is offering a standard which is itself objective, making no reference to the *agent's* actual or even idealized psychology, it (1) falls prey to the *action-ownership* problem, and (2) when we try to use the standard to construct a rule or principle that is action-guiding, it even just gives us the wrong results. But Jackson is putting words in Railton's mouth when he pushes this criticism, and I return to this issue later in the book when I discuss Jackson's view that objective consequentialism – or, rather, Railton's version in which good moral agents are committed to the objective consequentialist standard – provides the wrong answers regarding what agents ought to do.

For now, to support Railton's claim let's consider what the action-guiding criticism comes down to. There is a very trivial sense in which a standard is not action-guiding because standards aren't the sorts of things that guide action. But this is too easy a criticism. The response is simply that, of course, the standard itself doesn't guide action but can be *utilized* to guide action. But the standard still has evaluative priority because the action that conforms to the standard is the right one – whether or not the person so acting was trying to conform to the standard.

1.2 More on friendship

Railton was primarily concerned with the practical problem that confronted consequentialists with respect to friendship and how to make that compatible with consequentialism. On objective consequentialism friendship can be justified independently of the agent's motivation and independently of evaluations of the agent's particular actions, even.

The 'friendship' criticism itself takes varying forms. Consequentialism:

1   commits moral agents to treating friends as mere means to maximizing agent-neutral value;
2   commits the moral agent to regulating his friendships according to consequentialist norms; and/or
3   views the value of friendship itself as instrumental.

Consider the first form of the criticism, which Railton's account nicely meets. The idea behind (1) is that the consequentialist is committed to using a consequentialist decision-procedure, or is committed to acting on pure consequentialist motivation to promote overall well-being. On this crude picture, then, the consequentialist moral agent always consciously acts to maximize the good and this is incompatible with taking a friend to be an *end in herself*, and treating her accordingly. Neera Badhwar puts the problem the following way:

> A consequentialist agent is required to justify his friendships – as all his other values – as a means to the maximal good. Apparently, then, from the impersonal *moral* point of view he can value his friendships only in instrumental terms, and this suggests that his moral commitments are psychologically incompatible with the attitudes and motivations of end friendship.[10]

This is the sort of objection that Railton's distinction is meant to handle. Consequentialism, objective consequentialism, holds the rightness of actions to depend upon the actual consequences produced by the action relative to available alternatives. But it sets an objective standard, and requires no particular consequentialist *psychology*. In maximizing the good the agent needn't expect, intend, or realize she is maximizing the good and her action would still be the right action. Thus, it might well be the case that the good friend acts well – in such a way that is part of a system that maximizes the good – and acts explicitly on norms of love or friendship, treating the loved one as an end in herself and not merely as a means.

Railton illustrates this by discussing two contrasting cases. One is the case of John and Anne, and the other is the case of Juan and Linda. John is married to Anne, and he is also a committed consequentialist. He is directly motivated by consequentialist concerns, so that when he does nice things for Anne he justifies the actions by appealing to consequentialist considerations. As Railton puts it, when a friend of John's compliments him on his affection for Anne, John responds: "I've always thought that people should help each other when they're in a specially good position to do so. I know Anne better than anyone else does, so I know better what she wants and needs. Besides, I have such affection for her that it's no great burden – instead, I get a lot of satisfaction out of it. Just think how awful marriage would be, or life itself, if people didn't take special care of the ones they love."[11] Note the reasons cited are impartialist and point to the utility – in terms of happiness – that is generated by the loving relationship. To critics of consequentialism this looks off-putting.

But compare John to Juan, who is a *sophisticated* consequentialist, one who recognizes the disutility of always thinking and deliberating along consequentialist lines, and who, instead, as discussed earlier, regards the duty to maximize agent-neutral value as a *regulative ideal*. That is, it sets a standard by which it is good and useful to compare one's actions, but does not offer a decision-procedure to guide all of one's actions and doesn't set the morally appropriate content of the good moral agent's motives. Juan is married to Linda. Juan loves Linda very much. He engages in many activities that support his relationship with Linda, and Linda herself. Juan is also personally committed to moral values. He does think that people ought to act for the best, but he also thinks that one needn't always think in consequentialist terms. When he is complimented on his relationship, as John was, his response is: "I love Linda. I even *like* her. So it means a lot to me to do things for her. After all we've been through, it is almost a part of me to do it." When challenged on the level of commitment to consequentialism he responds: "Look, it's a better world when people can have a relationship like ours – and nobody could if everyone were always asking themselves who's got the most need. It's not easy to make things work in this world, and one of the best things that happens to people is to have a close relationship like ours. You'd make things worse in a hurry if you broke up those close relationships for the sake of some higher goal."[12]

Juan, the sophisticated consequentialist, first responds to the compliment by noting his love for his wife. It was only when challenged that he brought consequentialist reasoning itself to bear in justifying his love for his wife, and the partial norms that underlie this offer a regulative ideal for him, a standing commitment for him, it is something that is still part of his psyche, though not part of his deliberations when he is interacting with his wife. In this way, the sophisticated consequentialist avoids being alienated from the standard that justifies his own actions. Another thing that Railton notes about Juan is that he has dispositions to do certain things that are part of a utility-maximizing system, but that do not call for motives with 'utility maximization' as content. Railton here is recognizing that we can distinguish act evaluation from character evaluation, and that the objective consequentialist is free to say that the action is wrong, though it stems from a good disposition, a disposition that, overall, is very good for people to have, given objective consequentialist standards. This approach to consequentialist friendship has been criticized because it seems incompatible with what Dean Cocking and Justin Oakley term the appropriate 'terminating' conditions for friendship. Even the sophisticated consequentialist, in one of her reflective moments, would terminate a friendship if it failed to live up to the consequentialist standard. As Railton himself notes, the sophisticated consequentialist's "motivational structure meets a counterfactual condition: while he ordinarily does not do what he does simply for the sake of doing what is right, he would seek to live a different sort of life if he did not think it was morally defensible."[13] But friendship requires a deeper commitment, they contend, and is incompatible with this terminating condition. Linda would feel just as alienated as Anne on discovering that Juan is willing to terminate their relationship when it fails to maximize the good, even though this is simply a guiding consideration, and does not form a part of any of his motives in interacting with Linda.

There are at least two responses available to the sophisticated consequentialist. First, Elinor Mason argues that Railton's view is not about terminating relationships on the basis of a consequentialist standard. Rather, Railton is talking about changing pro-friendship dispositions if one discovers those dispositions are in fact incompatible with one's living a morally defensible life. This would be much more difficult to do, and could only be undertaken in unusual circumstances.[14]

Another response is to simply note that Railton has made an empirical mistake about what leads to the best outcomes vis-à-vis friendship, but that this in no way affects the standard. Rather, it simply shows that it may well be best if people ignore consequentialism, at least when it comes to close personal relationships. The problem is that for the sophisticated consequentialist the consequentialist standard is still something that she has in mind as a regulative ideal. It may be that one is a better person if one lacks any conscious commitment to the consequentialist standard. This strategy would not be preferred by Railton because it, in effect, gives up on the alienation problem by holding that it may turn out that we ought to be alienated. In his early work on self-effacingness of theories, Derek Parfit noted that the point of a moral theory is not to be accepted, it is to be true. Consequentialism can provide the right standard, even if believing in that standard undermines one's ability to live a morally good life.

This sophisticated consequentialist solution to the alienation problem also has implications for how consequentialism approaches the demandingness problem. The demandingness problem comes up again if we take consequentialism to require pervasive impartiality in such a way that requires we reject personal relationships if and when those relationships fail to maximize the good. Yet, if one argues as Railton does, that sophisticated consequentialism does not, in fact, require this, then this aspect of the demandingness problem is avoided.

But some writers have pointed out that this type of strategy – that of treating consequentialism as merely a standard, rather than as also providing a decision-procedure or an account of practical reasons – is defective because it fails a crucial desideratum of a moral theory. That is, the argument goes, it fails to provide an account of an agent having *decisive* moral reasons to act or not act in a certain way. Paul Hurley argues, for example, that indirect strategies like Railton's sophisticated consequentialist strategy may reduce demandingness by allowing scope for personal relationships, but then the resulting theory is not demanding *enough*.[15] If consequentialism sets only a standard of 'right' then it is possible that one could hold that the right action maximizes the good, impartially considered, but that one does not have decisive reason to do what is morally right. In effect, he charges, this is what the sophisticated consequentialist is claiming. The right action for Juan would be to send money to Oxfam rather than spend the money visiting his wife, Linda, but he does not have decisive reason to do so, since he is allowed to act on the basis of personal preference. If this is the case, then, in principle, objective consequentialism would allow for views in which the standard is demanding as a standard, but since it does not provide decisive reasons for adhering to the standard itself, it is not at all demanding in practice. If this is true, then a theory of standards-consequentialism needs some sort of supplementation to get around the problem of not being demanding enough. Such a theory needs to provide a rationale for:

(DR) We have decisive reason to avoid moral wrongdoing.[16]

Without some rationale for (DR) the theory can't account for any rational pressure to conform behavior to the consequentialist standard.

One way to avoid this problem is to deny that, strictly speaking, (DR) is true. When discussing the satisficing alternative to maximization, for example, we saw that in order to avoid demandingness some writers believed that it made sense to hold that we always have sufficient reason to maximize the good but we are not always required to do so. This seemed completely irrational, given that one was thinking along a single continuum of good, along which reasons for action are understood. But suppose that we distinguish types of reasons, moral reasons being only one such type, and then deny that moral reasons are overriding? We might, for example, hold that personal relationships provide reasons that are, by their very nature, partial rather than impartial, and that these relationships generate a separate class of reasons for action that are weighty in their own right.[17] Hurley dismisses this strategy:

> Such an approach ... only wins this strategic battle by losing the war so many consequentialists have taken themselves to be fighting. A central aim of many consequentialists has been to demonstrate that we should be doing more than moderate morality requires of us. But the approach in question lowers the bar of rational demands to act morally even as it raises the bar of moral standards. ... If we accept that morality, properly understood, provides merely one among other sets of standards and that these standards lack the distinctive relationship that has been claimed for them to our reasons for acting, then morality is shifted toward the margins in meaningful inquiry about what we have good reasons to do. This would be a Pyrrhic victory, vindicating consequentialist morality only by marginalizing the role of morality in practical reason and deliberation.[18]

This is not true. The view that moral reasons are only one sort of reason and that moral reasons do not override all other reasons does not lead to 'anything goes' and an abandonment of the significance of moral reasons to practical deliberation. Moral reasons, even if not 'overriding' or 'decisive', will still carry great weight. There are of course issues on how, exactly, to weigh different reasons.

One possible avenue is to appeal to an intuition prevalent in 'common-sense' morality that different sorts of value support different sorts of normative considerations. It may be that goods such as hedonic well-being and accomplishment, with respect to the *self*, constitute distinctly prudential reasons and that hedonic well-being and accomplishment with respect to *others* are moral. This would be to embrace the self/other asymmetry that consequentialism has historically denied.

Another worry about standards-consequentialism, however, is that it simply raises a different kind of alienation problem. The factors, or reasons, that justify the agent's actions may not be the reasons the agent himself has in mind in performing those actions. Reasons of love, for example, do *not* appeal to maximizing utility. Consider the woman who is helping her child with a school project, or taking him to a play, or baking him a birthday cake. Her deliberations do not take the form: "It is good for parents to favor their children since this favoring, overall, promotes the good." Rather, with each activity, she is simply thinking about helping her child, or doing something nice for him. It is good to *act on* such reasons because they maximize utility, but this is not part of the agent's calculation, or the agent's actual delib-eration. Thus, the agent is 'alienated' from the true justification of his own action.

But insisting that the agent be cognizant at the time of action when it comes to the factors that justify the action, and explicitly and consciously act on those reasons, poses a different set of problems. It seems wildly unrealistic, and fails to reflect how normal people go about behaving in ways that are intuitively admirable. The villagers in Le Chambon, France, for example, risked their own lives to save Jewish children from the Nazis for reasons that they found difficult to articulate and even identify. We view their behavior as very admirable because we believe that in acting this way they were responding to the right sorts of reasons – that the suffering of innocents should be prevented – even though the reasons cited were explic-itly religious, rather than ones that cited universal moral norms.

This undercuts an observation about admirability that is fairly common-place. That is the view that one gets moral credit for following rules and principles rather than merely acting in accordance with rules and prin-ciples. Consider the imperative 'Don't eat meat' that rests on 'Eating meat is wrong'. Janice would normally like to eat meat, but is persuaded that it is wrong to do so, so she refrains from eating it. Janice is following the rule that proscribes eating meat, and thus deserves moral credit. Marie, on the other hand, has no views on the morality of meat eating but just doesn't like meat. Marie also refrains from eating meat, but not because she is following the rule. Rather, she is simply acting in such a way that her behavior accords with what the rule proscribes. She gets no moral credit, the thought goes, even though her actual behavior is indistinguish-able from Janice's. But this view doesn't withstand more careful scru-tiny. The reason why such emphasis is placed on rule following, critics would argue, is that for persons who lack the appropriate dispositions such guidance is necessary for success. But that doesn't mean that it is necessary across the board. To say that it is following the rule that is both necessary and sufficient is saying something much more than that, and turning a teleological theory of the right into a procedural one. Again, one can bring out the rule worship objection, that rule following can lead to irrational action in cases where the good to be maximized clearly entails violating the rule in question.

What does seem important is that there be a connection to the will, to the agent's psychology in some respect, so that the disposition in question has a psychological basis.[19] Consider a kind of curmudgeonly character who is a bit Scrooge-like in some of his avowed beliefs and attitudes. He believes, and says he believes, that poor people simply need to knuckle down and get to work. On the other hand, he regularly gives to charity out of sincere feelings of sympathy for the sufferings of the poor. In spite of beliefs that seem rather awful, his regular and consistent charitable behavior indicates that he is responsive to the right reasons.[20]

Thus, rather than rule following, the important thing is that the agent be responsive to the right sorts of reasons even if she isn't thinking of them at the time of action (or, even, at all). This isn't to dismiss the importance of rule following. Rules of thumb are very important as heuristics that help guide action efficiently, reducing the costs of deliberation.

Some recent work in social psychology supports the view that people often act on reasons that they are not consciously aware of.[21] Further, when people are asked to reconstruct their reasoning, *post hoc*, they often confabulate. Joshua Greene and Jonathan Haidt discuss some psychological studies regarding this tendency to manufacture a deliberative process that is not, in fact, followed: "People certainly do engage in moral reasoning, but, as suggested by studies of informal reasoning these processes are typically one-sided efforts in support of pre-ordained conclusions."[22] Their conclusion is that many of our decisions are the result of automatic processes. 'Automatic' is, in many ways, an unfortunate choice of word here. Automatic actions are norm-governed; it's just that they are not deliberative. Neither are they reflexive. Yawning and blinking are not automatic in this sense of the word. However, the norms governing the automatic action might well not be directly accessible to the agent performing the action. Even when they are, agents seem to have a tendency to manufacture narratives about their own behavior that conform to their self-image. This is an example of confabulation.

Reasons confabulation is commonplace. People are often asked to justify their actions, or explain the normative considerations that prompted them, and they grasp for reasons that seem to make sense. Often this is guided by the person's view of his own character. The agent picks the sorts of reasons that fit nicely with what someone with that sort of character would do. This raises some doubt as to how much deliberation moral agents really do engage in, as well as their ability to pick out the reasons that actually moved them to act. On the view of virtue I have advocated elsewhere, what is most important to our judgment of moral character is the reasons that guide the agent, regardless of whether the agent is in a position herself to identify those reasons and articulate them cogently.

Evidence of confabulation is extensive. While a good deal of the literature focuses on people who have clinical psychological conditions, there is
some work on normal human reasoners as well.[23] Confabulation involves
the making of a sincere judgment that is very poorly grounded in evidence;
such judgments are widely believed to be epistemic errors. The psychology
literature has tended to focus on a tendency to embellish one's memories –
adding details that are actually absent from the original experience. While
confabulations can be associated with morally bad behaviors, they can also
be associated with morally good ones. A person might misrepresent her
own motivations to herself in order to act well, for example. The cases that
interest us here are cases, for example, where a person's theory of the self
influences how she views her own behavior and motivations, contrary to
the evidence. Lisa Bortolotti and Rochelle E. Cox have hypothesized that the
automatic making up of details in one's experience may support the development of positive self-images – or the "sense of self."[24] In any case, this
self-construction can be either good or bad, morally speaking. The really
interesting feature of confabulation is that cases of morally good behavior
can display it, and thus it would seem that morally good behavior can
survive the agent's mistaken view of her own motivations. What really justifies a person's actions is the extent to which they conform to the standard of
right. What makes a person morally praiseworthy or morally blameworthy
are the reasons their actions are responsive to – even when the agents themselves mislocate their own motivating reasons. If Huckleberry Finn was
really responding in a sympathetic way to his friend Jim's suffering, he was
acting well – even if he himself did not see it that way.[25] In the psychology
literature 'confabulation' is reserved for interpretation of *past* mental states.
Confabulations are then contrasted with 'introspective' reports. Introspective
reports of our conscious thoughts are themselves thought to be reliable –
but reliable simply as reports of our thoughts. The issue that mainly concerns
me is another sort of reliability – reliability regarding access to reasons for
actions. An agent may be reliably reporting at the time of action what she
thinks is motivating her, true, but may not be a reliable reporter of what
actually motivates her. Confabulation shows that people make up elements
of what they were really thinking in the past, and there is another body of
evidence that indicates a different kind of error as well, a misidentification
of motivating reasons not only with respect to past behavior but also with
respect to present behavior.

Of course, one could hold that the normative theory we are discussing
prescribes, and so needn't be subject to any information regarding how

people actually go about making moral choices, how they actually behave. But what seems more plausible is to hold that we view people as responsible if they are responsive to the right sorts of reasons, even if they cannot clearly articulate, express, or clearly represent those reasons to themselves. They may be able to, after long and careful reflection on their attitudes and behavior, but, then, they may not be able to, either, and still be regarded as morally good agents who have acted rightly.

Thus, we can make a distinction between character and act in moral evaluation. The action is right when it maximizes the good, though the agent may or may not be acting from a good character, or a virtue. This allows for a much more nuanced account of moral evaluation. Indeed, one needn't stop at action and character. Global consequentialists hold that the consequentialist evaluative standard be applied to anything relating to agency (or actually, anything at all, though there will be a good many practical reasons for limiting such evaluation to factors relevant to agency). This would include motives and intentions, as well as action and dispositions such as character traits. For now we will focus on action, but return to global consequentialism later. The view that I argue for is that action evaluation does not have across-the-board primacy in our evaluative practices. That is determined by the context of the evaluation. Good arguments can be given as to why, historically, we have focused more on action evaluation, but that is largely a historical artifact.[26] Further, whatever the mode of evaluation used, the correct account is consequentialist. What makes a motive good is the effects associated with it; what makes a character trait good is its effects; and so forth.

The objective consequentialist account of right action views actions as evaluated according to their outcomes, independent of particular features of the agent's psychology. But, as I'll spell out in more detail later, these two features can be pulled apart. To solve the fundamental problems Railton sets out to solve with the notion of objective consequentialism, one need only hold that the act be evaluated according to a standard that is not necessarily reflected in the agent's actual psychology.

We should note several possibilities here. Subjective consequentialism can be spelled out, in principle, in a variety of ways. One could hold that the right action is the action the agent hopes produces the best outcome, or doubts will produce the best outcome, or fears will produce the best outcome. But none of these is at all plausible. They define right action in terms of the agent having a certain subjective mental state with respect to optimal outcomes, but, we know, empirically, that the relevant psychological state has to do with the agent's expectations, or what the agent actually foresees will produce the best outcome. Thus, the following general formulation is often given as an account that is a fairly good example of subjective consequentialism with respect to act evaluation:

> (EUS) The right action is the action the agent *expects* will produce the most good and/or least bad among the agent's alternatives.

Note that in (EUS) what determines the rightness of the action is the agent's subjective state. (EUS) can be formulated either so that the agent needs to be consciously trying to maximize the good, or simply so that the agent's expectations about what will happen in the future, plus her normative commitments, determine the right action. The latter is much more plausible, since the former, as we discussed in Chapter 2, is actually a form of 'deliberationism'.

How can we spell out the difference between subjective and objective? We can contrast objective with subjective by holding that the right action is the one that actually produces the most good, regardless of whether the agent is trying to do so. This is the actual outcomes formulation:

> (AO) The right action is the action that produces the most good and/or the least bad amongst the options open to the agent at the time of action.

Or the contrast is that the objective consequentialist holds that the right action is determined by factors independent of the agent's actual psychology – so the contrast is between a criterion that is *actually* subjective and one that is not. For example, the foreseeable consequences formulation holds that:

> (FO) The right action is the action that produces the most foreseeable good and/or least bad amongst the options open to the agent at the time of action.

Since 'foreseeable' is not the same as 'foreseen', (FO) is not appealing to the agent's actual subjective states in defining right action, and thus this is not an example of subjective consequentialism. However, (FO) still provides an evidence-sensitive standard. What matters are the outcomes that are foresee*able*. Of course, note that a good deal of weight is placed on 'foreseeable'. However, some might argue that (FO) isn't really objective, since it doesn't define right action in terms of actual outcomes of the action. Again, the standard is evidence-sensitive even if it doesn't appeal to what the agent actually believes. On my view, what is significant about objective consequentialism is that it divorces the standard of evaluation from the agent's actual psychology. While it is true that this is often taken to imply that the standard must therefore be the actual outcomes, this isn't necessarily the case.

Further, (FO) can be articulated in ways that index the standard to the agent. There may not be much difference between (AO) and (FO) if 'foreseeable' is understood as 'foreseeable by the ideal observer' — that is, someone who is fully informed and perfectly impartial in assessing the good. The problem with (AO) and with a version of (FO) that has been spelled out this way is that it seems that the standard is utterly inaccessible. Since effects of our actions continue long after our own lives are over, after the end of the world itself, even, is there even such a thing as a right action? Yes, there are actions that are right, but we are not in a position to know which actions are right because we do not know what is actually going to happen in the distant future, nor do we have a way of knowing. Thus the problem is epistemic. It is this problem that has pushed people to opt for a standard that is at least indexed to the subject. Again, though, this doesn't mean that one needs to appeal to the agent's actual psychology in fully spelling out the standard of right. It may be that the knowledge problem is overblown. One possibility is that 'right' is context-sensitive and that (AO) needs to be spelled out in this light. Alastair Norcross, for example, has argued that the unforeseeable future problem can be handled.[27] This is because it is always morally appropriate, morally right, to make the choice on the basis of the foreseeable, even if there are factors that are morally relevant, which one knows one cannot foresee. Norcross uses the following case to illustrate:

> [Y]ou are visiting a totalitarian dictatorship on a humanitarian mission, when the dictator himself, whom you have reason to trust, informs you that the fates of two political prisoners of conscience, Smith and Jones, are in your hands. You can specify whether Smith lives or dies. If you do not specify either fate for Smith, you will be taken to have specified death. In addition, you are told that the fate of Jones is tied to your decision about Smith. At this very moment, in a different part of the presidential palace, a coin is being tossed to link your decision about Smith to a decision about Jones. If the coin lands heads, life for Smith will also mean life for Jones, and death for Smith will mean death for Jones. If the coin lands tails, life for Smith will mean death for Jones, and death for Smith will mean life for Jones. You will not learn of the result of the coin toss.

It's clear that in this case the decision should be life for Smith, given that all you have to worry about are these two individuals. But Norcross also asks about a case where a third person's fate is added. In the more complicated scenario – where, again, the unknown outcome of the coin toss determines the fates of two other individuals besides Smith – it is *possible* that choosing for Smith has a worse outcome. One just doesn't know. So the decision should still be in favor of saving Smith. Though Norcross doesn't explicitly point this out, it is also the case that things would of course change if you did know, or find out, what the coin toss result was. So there is clearly a sense of 'right' tied to objective outcomes. But this is also clearly divorced from the issue of what you should do under the circumstances.

1.2 The subjective version

As noted earlier, the subjective version can be spelled out in a wide variety of ways. Do we formulate the criterion on the basis of what the agent actually expects, or what the agent, given her actual beliefs, should expect? We can draw on the literature on epistemic possibility to highlight what is at stake. Consider this case, modified from a case of Ian Hacking's:

> (S) Steve is searching for a sunken ship. He has copies of the ship's log, and on the basis of the information in the log calculates the location of the wreck as lying in a bay to the north. However, Steve has made a miscalculation, and in reality the wreck is over 30 miles from the bay in which he expects to find the ship.[28]

Steve certainly believes it is possible that the ship is in the northern bay, and, more than that, he fully expects it to be there. Indeed, he has this expectation on the basis of what he considers good evidence, but he simply makes a miscalculation on the basis of that evidence and comes to a conclusion regarding the location of the ship that is not, in fact, a possible location.[29] On the basis of what Steve expects, he is right to go to the northern bay; on the basis of what he expects, given consideration of the evidence, he is right to go to the northern bay; but on the basis of the evidence as it should have been utilized, using proper calculations, and thus, on the basis of what he should have expected given his actual evidence, he is wrong to go to the northern bay.

The general issue is that, in order for the subjective view to remain a plausible account of 'right' it needs *some* constraint on the basis of evidence, on the basis of what is reasonable for the agent to believe. Otherwise, people with extremely unreasonable views that are not at all supported by the evidence available to *them* end up acting rightly. Suppose Alex believes that the best use of her charitable contributions is to support groups that condone the killing of all persons who disagree with her political views. She is seriously mistaken about this, there is no evidence that this would be good, and plenty of evidence that it would be bad. But if the final court of moral appeal is just what Alex happens to believe, then on the radical subjective view this course of action is 'right'. But this, at least intuitively, seems incorrect, although some theorists seem willing to condone this since they view 'right' as what is 'right' in the agent's own eyes. But even writers who make this move, such as Frank Jackson, note they have a problem with cases of negligent ignorance. Usually, then, they add a duty to acquire reliable information to the account, so that the person who is negligent may be said to, strictly speaking, act rightly, but in a way that is still blameworthy if he fails to exert himself to acquire reliable information.

Another way to go, that doesn't tag on this extra duty, is to make some reference to conformity to evidence in the account of right action itself. This would be an *evidence-sensitive* subjective account of right action. Again, there are different levels of sensitivity. If the account ties 'right' to evidence the agent actually is aware of, then some of the counterintuitive implications of the simple subjective view can be avoided, but not all. However, if the account ties 'right' to evidence the agent isn't actually aware of, but which is available to her – for example, if only she were to read the newspaper, or be minimally attentive to the world around her – then the account is moving further away from the spirit of the subjective approach, which was to capture the sense of 'right' by 'the agent's own lights'.

How are we to interpret the addition, made by writers like Jackson, to acquire information? Jackson believes that this duty is explicated by appeal to what it is useful for the agent to do, and getting more information is certainly useful:

> Getting more information and then doing what has greatest moral utility has itself greatest moral utility provided the possible change in utility consequent on the new information when weighed by the probability of getting that new information is great enough to compensate for the effort and cost of getting the new information.[30]

He then appeals to a proof Paul Horwich provides to this effect.[31] This seems very plausible. However, it doesn't solve the problem for Jackson, or any other consequentialist who believes that the agent's own beliefs are what set the standard of rightness. This is because the appeal to the duty to get more information rests on the view that more information is beneficial. This seems reasonable, but it also seems entirely possible for an agent to fail to believe this, and, indeed, actually believe the opposite. Consider someone, Leslie, who believes that new information simply clutters the mind, and leads to confusion. Leslie fails to try to acquire new information because of this belief she has about information itself, and its failure to be useful. On the account Jackson is promoting it would seem that Leslie does not have a duty to get more information – and the problem of negligent ignorance is simply pushed back a level.

The further away the subjective account moves from reference to the agent's own state of mind at the time of action, the further away it gets from providing an action-guiding standard. Many writers have noted that (OC) doesn't seem to do well when it comes to action guidance, and thus some version of (EUS) needs to take center stage – that the subjective account can be action-guiding. This is one main reason why people move from (OC) to the expected utility version of the theory. But as Fred Feldman has pointed out, if one is motivated to move to (EUS) by a concern for action guidance, one's hopes will be unfulfilled. Feldman notes that writers who opt for the 'expected utility' formulation avoid reference to the agent's own expected utility and opt, instead, for something like:

> (PCU) An action A is *right* if and only if A has as high an expected utility as any alternative action that the agent could perform instead.

Feldman is discussing Mark Timmons' view in which (PCU) is offered as a decision-procedure for the consequentialist, and as a way of meeting the action-guiding criterion. If one follows (PCU) one will not be blameworthy. Thus, this is really a criticism of viewing something like the expected utility criterion as a guide for blameworthiness rather than 'right' action itself. But the problem with viewing it as a criterion of blameworthiness carries over to the criterion of 'right'. As Feldman notes, (PCU) is not a realistic action-guiding procedure. Actually calculating expected utilities amongst a range of options in even fairly straightforward cases will be enormously complex. It isn't something people would be able to do in most situations.

Another issue has to do with the way alternatives are to be determined. Fleshing out both (EUS) and many versions of (OC) requires that we state the right action is the one with the best effects, *amongst the alternatives open to the agent*. Critics of the objective version of the theory sometimes overlook this very important clause. For example, subjective consequentialists such as Frances Howard-Snyder and Elinor Mason criticize the objective theory for its impracticality. They argue that the standard violates the 'ought implies can' principle. The basic idea behind the subjective consequentialist strategy is to show that the objective consequentialist recommends actions that are *practically impossible.*

Frances Howard-Snyder uses an example of playing chess with Karpov to illustrate the problem. Suppose that something really wonderful would happen if Alice played chess with Karpov and won. The objective consequentialist will hold that the right thing for her to do is to play chess with Karpov and win, even though this is not realistic. It is not logically impossible, nor is it physically impossible, since Alice is able to move chess pieces around the board, nor is it psychologically impossible, let's say, since she knows the moves of the game. But because Karpov is so much better than Alice at chess, it is practically impossible, that is, impossible as a practical matter.

The general drift of the criticism is that if we view 'ought' or obligation as implying that the agent can maximize the good, then objective consequentialism does not satisfy this constraint. It doesn't satisfy the constraint because agents don't have the relevant kind of ability when it comes to maximizing the good. Mason writes:

> Consider objective consequentialism: even for objective consequentialism, 'maximize' should be interpreted as 'maximize within the bounds of what is physically and logically possible'. Thus agents can always maximize the good, and can always know that they can maximize the good. However, this is also useless. An agent has to identify a particular course of action, which would, if successfully performed, maximize the good. The instruction, 'maximize the good' is not action guiding unless the agent has some idea of what would maximize the good.[32]

But this criticism ignores the specification of alternatives. The objective consequentialist need only say that the right action is the one with the best outcomes amongst the set of alternatives open to the agent – and beating Karpov at chess is not an alternative open to the agent.

The criticism also ignores a basic distinction that most objective consequentialists subscribe to – the distinction, in some form, between criterion and decision-procedure; between the metaphysics and epistemology
of right. The right action is the one that maximizes the good. How we go
figuring out how to do this is a different issue. The criterion of evaluation
is the good. The best strategy for getting there might be to try to maximize the expected, or foreseen, good; or it might not. It might be rolling
dice, or reading the horoscope. These are not likely to be good-maximizing
decision-procedures, but it is an empirical issue.

Another way to understand what is at stake between the subjective and
objective consequentialist is to consider the differing standards used to evaluate theories. Subjective consequentialists conflate, on my view, the usefulness of the theory and the evidence in favor of the theory's truth. Of course,
they self-consciously engage in the conflation out of a belief that the true
moral theory must also be useful. The argument typically involves noting
that ethics is *practical*, and thus must provide a decision-procedure for people
to use in deciding how to act, and, further, the criterion for evaluation is
itself the use of the decision-procedure. Success is understood in terms of
sticking to the appropriate procedure. Consider the analogy with justice: an
outcome is just when the appropriate procedure is used to get the outcome,
even if a guilty person goes free or an innocent is condemned. There is
a sense of 'just' that corresponds to the procedural understanding, just as
there is a sense of 'right' that corresponds to the procedural understanding
promulgated by the subjective consequentialists. But these understandings
are understood completely relative to the success standard. If the procedure is shown to deviate dramatically away from success, the procedure is
changed. It is perverse to change the standard of 'success' of getting it 'right'
– of guilt and innocence – in light of pre-identification of a procedure.

On the view that I am suggesting, the objective version of the theory
(whether it be (AO) or (FO)) is correct, though (EUS) may be more useful
as the outline of a decision-procedure to actually employ in trying to live
up to the theory so that one's actions come as close as possible to hitting the
target specified by the theory. Again, that is an empirical issue, but as long as
we recognize that decision-procedures are themselves evaluated relative to
contexts of use, it seems very plausible that (EUS) provides a good procedure for many contexts in which rules of thumb are too vague or indeter-
minate. Further, we can then see (EUS), or, more likely, (FO) as providing
a *standard* for something other than 'rightness' – such as praiseworthiness. If
the agent performs the action she (reasonably) expects will maximise the

good amongst her options, then she is praiseworthy even if that is no guar-
antee of being right.

How do we test whether an action meets the standard of rightness? Some
argue that we can use a simple subjunctive test — a is the right action iff
option a would have the best effects amongst the action options open to
the agent at the time of choice. This means that if the agent, S, performs a
rather than b at time t, a is the right action iff the outcome of performing a
is better than what would have happened if the agent had performed b. To
assess this we need to make a judgment about what would have happened
if the agent had performed b instead. So, we consider the closest possible
world in which the agent does b rather than a. If the effects are worse then
the agent acted rightly in performing a instead.

This simple formulation is highly intuitive, and seems to capture how we
think about the best choice among alternative courses of action. But problems have been raised concerning counterintuitive results about the oblig-
atoriness of actions which are themselves part of more complex actions.
Suppose Mary gives to Oxfam rather than buys a new stereo. Giving to Oxfam
involves reaching into her desk drawer to get her checkbook, filling out the
check, putting it in an envelope, addressing the envelope, finding a stamp ...
and so forth. We can judge her to have done the right thing since giving to
Oxfam has better effects than buying a new stereo. She was thus obligated
to give to Oxfam. But does it follow that she was also obligated to reach into
her desk drawer? That sounds rather odd, yet it also seems true that if she had
not done so the alternative would have been worse, since reaching into the
desk was a necessary step in sending the money to Oxfam in this instance.

This can be dealt with, however, by relativizing right judgments to action
descriptions. We might dub this a semantic solution. So, "Mary is obligated
to give to Oxfam" is true, understood in the context in which giving the
money to Oxfam, rather than buying a new stereo, is maximally good-
producing. "Mary is obligated to reach into her desk drawer" is also true,
as long as it is understood against the background of performing an action
that is maximally productive of the good. Why it sounds odd is that such an
utterance doesn't wear its maximally good-producing quality on its sleeve,
so to speak. When one reaches into a drawer one could be on the way
to doing all kinds of other tasks: finding a birthday card, getting a pencil
sharpener, and so forth. Once the judgments are properly understood in
context, then, the oddity disappears. It is no odder than saying something
like "You ought to put your shoes on since you ought to take a walk now"
when one needs to put one's shoes on in order to take the walk.

Some, however, suggest a modal test that involves a more direct rank ordering of possible worlds. Probably the best-known version of this is Fred Feldman's. He argues that the agent ought to perform the action *a* just in case the agent performs that action, *a*, in the *best* worlds accessible to the agent at the time of action performance.[33]

Why would anyone choose (FO) over (AO)? (AO), after all, seems much more theoretically pure. (FO), however, is tempting because it solves a major problem for the theory – the problem of how to restrict the scope of the relevant consequences. If we don't do this somehow, then really there's never been a right action, let alone a right action that we actually know about. James Lenman pushes this objection to objective consequentialism.[34] Lenman notes that many of our moral decisions will have 'identity'-affecting outcomes. Thus, if a company, for example, decides to reduce the amount of pollution it offloads into a river, this decision will affect the identities of those living in the future. Different people will exist than otherwise would have existed, and these people will in turn make different decisions. This means that – given enough time – we won't be able to predict outcomes, and thus won't be able to know what action amongst the options open to us is the best outcome. Of course, the full problem with objective consequentialism is more severe: it would follow from that view that there is no right action *so far*, which seems very implausible. However, if we argue that the right action is that action that produces the best in terms of *foreseeable* outcomes, then this doesn't follow. The scope of relevant outcomes is fixed by what is foreseeable for the agent. This is one reason, then, for opting for (FO) over (AO).

But this problem loses its bite when we consider that the future is real, not something which, at this point, is not real. The view that holds that on the (AO) view there are no right actions because there is no future would be undercut. So, (AO) can avoid this particular criticism. Often those who make this criticism are really worried about the epistemological concern that we won't be able to tell which action really is the right action because of our epistemic limitations: we are not able to see into the future, certainly not able to infer into the future with perfect accuracy. But this is a separate worry. (AO) is giving an account of what 'right action' means, either a semantic account or a metaphysical one, about what right actions *are*. How we go about figuring out which action is right is a different, though interesting, issue. Further, (FO) itself does not offer a perfect solution to the epistemological worries. There will still be the problem of how to figure out the 'foreseeable' – people will often make mistakes that affect their judgment about which action is the right action. That doesn't make it the case that there is no right action, however.

Thus, these worries about (AO) can be met.

1.3 Moral luck

Another issue that pushes a good many people to reject objective consequentialism in favor of subjective consequentialism is the problem of moral luck. Consider (AO). On this view it is what actually happens in the world that determines the rightness or wrongness of the action. This makes the moral quality of the action very much subject to luck factors.

Thus, the problem of moral luck notes the fundamental tension between, on the one hand, holding people responsible only for the contents of their wills and, on the other, holding them responsible for what actually happens as a result of their actions. We are used to thinking that if a person intends harm to another and isn't actually incompetent, then one can reasonably expect the harm to occur. However, moral luck cases famously point out that often our success or failure is due to factors beyond our control. Thomas Nagel makes this point in the following passage:

> However jewel-like the good will may be in its own right, there is a morally significant difference between rescuing someone from a burning building and dropping him from a twelfth-storey window while trying to rescue him. Similarly, there is a morally significant difference between reckless driving and manslaughter. But whether a reckless driver hits a pedestrian depends on the presence of the pedestrian at the point where he recklessly passes a red light.[35]

Many writers analyze the problem in terms of a 'control' condition on holding responsible. We hold people responsible only for things that are in their control, and what actually happens, as opposed to what the agent intends to happen, is not something the agent has ultimate control over. (AO) is a version of evaluational externalism, which holds that the moral quality of a person's action, or character, is determined by factors external to agency, such as the consequences of the action, or character trait, in question. (EUS) is an example of evaluational internalism, which holds that the moral quality of an action, or character, is determined by factors internal to agency, such as motives or intentions. Internalist accounts of evaluation – such as the subjective consequentialist offers – might well agree with

Nagel's claim above, but not view this as a problem for moral worth. It is a theoretical strength of the subjective position that it insulates moral evaluation from luck. Hence the challenge for externalist accounts, such as (AO).

The intuition elicited in the above case seems to be that if the reckless driver truly had no control over the presence of a person in the road, if the presence of the person was actually due to bad luck, he does not deserve extra blame for running over that person. The idea is that since the psychology is the same, and that's all the agent is controlling here, then the moral quality of the actions, and the level of blame, should be the same as well. But (AO) holds our actions hostage to moral luck.

Suppose that Mary is speeding, ever so slightly, as she drives to work one morning, but she has the bad luck to turn a corner just as a small child runs into the road.[36] She hits the child, and the child is injured. Contrast this case with another exactly like it in all respects except that the driver, in this case Albert, happened to arrive five minutes before the child ran into the street, and so did not harm anyone. Intuitively, most people find Mary's action horribly wrong, and Albert's merely somewhat wrong. And yet, independent of luck considerations, there is no difference. In terms of their psychology, they are identical. Further, they have no control over the effects of their actions, ultimately. The only thing a person has full control over is their intentions and motivational sets. On the full-bore objective view, since Mary's act led to worse effects than Albert's, Mary's act is morally worse. But, again, this seems quite odd since the psychology is the same. To avoid this oddity, one can adopt the subjective version of the theory. For example, consider (EUS). Since the agent has control over her intentions to try to produce the most good, on this view there is no morally relevant difference between Mary and Albert. They are both equally blameworthy, and the actions equally bad. But what the objective consequentialist does, the theorist who adopts (AO) instead, is to separate these two considerations. Mary and Albert may be equally blameworthy; they haven't performed equally bad actions.

Note that (FO) also does not have the same issue as (AO) with respect to luck. On this view, the moral quality of the action is determined by what is foreseeable, and praise and blame may or may not be tied to how closely the agent adheres to this standard – that depends on empirical factors having to do with the instrumental function of praise and blame. But this gives us at least a *prima facie* case for holding the agents equally wrong and equally blameworthy, even if there is a separate case to be made for a differential *holding* responsible. Combine this with the view that many of our ambivalent moral reactions to cases can in part be explained by the fact that we simultaneously evaluate different facets of an action – motive, intention, and so forth – and we can have an extremely nuanced, yet sometimes confusing way of evaluating what goes on with an action in a particular situation.

This strategy involves arguing for *global* consequentialism – that is, the view that we apply consequentialist evaluative criteria to more than actions. We *do*, in actual practice, evaluate more than the rightness or wrongness of *actions*. We also evaluate persons themselves as praiseworthy or blameworthy. We evaluate the mental states of agents. A person may act rightly in such a way as to reflect badly on her character; or she may act wrongly in such a way as to reflect well on her character.

All sorts of other pragmatic factors come into play in blaming someone. Since there seems little point in holding Joe responsible for what he would have done if he had lived in Germany in the 1930s – especially considering the epistemic obstacles to coming to a reliable judgment on such counterfactual matters – we don't normally engage in such speculations. We don't have access to the sort of information required for such speculations. In the case of the drivers, though, there may be some instrumental benefit. (FO) tells us that the agents in this case are equally wrong, and equally blameworthy, without appeal to their actual psychological states. By hypothesis, of course, one case is worse than the other, in terms of the actual state of affairs. Our tendency to hold the agent in the worse case more responsible may be irrational or arational (possibly because humans are very prone to focus on bad outcomes as a way of detecting moral 'cheaters ' in the community), or it is justified on the basis that it has an improving quality (i.e. its instrumental value).

One additional argument can be provided to support the objective view in these cases. This argument relies on the fact that there is a moral remainder in cases where an agent causes something bad to happen and becomes aware of it. That is, even if she realizes that she had no way of knowing that the bad effect would result, she feels very badly about it. The term 'remainder' refers to the feelings of remorse or agent-regret that survive reflection. When an agent feels bad for causing a bad outcome, though she did not anticipate it, she feels agent-regret, rather than remorse.[37] Remorse occurs when the agent feels a deeper responsibility – she knew the bad outcome was likely, or she should have known given the evidence available to her. Agent-regret is more intense than mere regret, which anyone might feel upon hearing about a misfortune suffered by others. Alice will regret the fact that children are suffering from malnutrition in other parts of the world, but she won't feel *agent*-regret unless she believes she was part of the cause (albeit unintentionally and/or unknowingly) of their suffering. That one feels agent-regret at all is puzzling, however, if, indeed, one lacks the psychology of the sort that subjectivists view as necessary for moral wrongdoing in these cases.

There are two choices when considering these feelings: either she ought to feel badly about the bad effects of her actions, or it is not the case that she ought to feel bad about the bad effects of her actions, worse than she would feel had she associated those effects with the actions of someone else.

Consider the case of the Schlegel sisters in E. M. Forster's *Howards End*.[38] The sisters try to help a clerk, Leonard Bast, avoid the ruin of his career by giving him information that they believe will help him avoid losing his job. However, through no fault of theirs, the information in fact turns out to be misleading, and in acting on it Mr. Bast ends up far worse off than he would have been. Judging the sisters purely on the basis of their psychology they are completely blameless. They were not negligent and they acted with the best of intentions. Yet they also feel very badly about how things worked out for Bast, far worse than they would have felt about it had they not been the cause of his career destruction. The objective consequentialist can diagnose this as a reasonable response. They ended up doing the wrong thing, even though they had no intention at all of hurting Bast. They have a natural desire to make some sort of amends, or gesture of support. The alternative is to view their extra level of distress as irrational in some way, something to be avoided and stamped out of existence, if possible. There are very many cases like this, in which blameless wrongdoers feel the need to make amends.

1.4 Action 'ownership'

There is another problem for objective consequentialism, the *action ownership problem*. Frank Jackson is critical of the objective approach because it divorces rightness from the agent too much:

> We need, if you like, a story from the inside of an agent to be part of any theory which is properly a theory in ethics, and having the best consequences is a story from the outside. It is fine for a theory in physics to tell us about its central notions in a way which leaves it obscure how to move from those notions to action, for that passage can be left to

something which is not physics: but the passage to action is the very business of ethics.[39]

Further, it leads to ridiculous conclusions about right action, since on Jackson's view the right one is at least in some cases not the best one.

He asks us to consider the case of Jill and John: Jill is a doctor, John her patient with a skin problem. Jill has two drugs available to treat the skin problem, X and Y. Drug X has a 90 percent chance of curing John, but a 10 percent chance of killing him. Drug Y has only a 50 percent chance of curing him, but no chance at all of killing him. Which should Jill prescribe?

> Railton's proposal is, I take it, that the moral decision problem should be approached by setting oneself the goal of doing what is objectively right – the action that in fact has the best consequences – and then performing the action which the empirical evidence suggests is most likely to have this property.[40]

Given this understanding of what the objective consequentialist is committed to, Jackson argues that the objective consequentialist will give the wrong answer in cases like the Jill and John case. Going for the best is a mistake. If one went with the option that had the highest probability of the best outcome it would be to give John drug X, which would be a terrible mistake. It is much too risky. Instead, we need to go with the action that has the best expected utility. That would be to prescribe drug Y, since drug Y has the best expected payoff. Often we need, morally, to 'play it safe' and this means that under conditions of uncertainty we don't opt for the course of action that is likeliest to have the best outcome. In unpacking 'maximize the good', it may be that the correct standard involves production of good, yes, but also avoidance of bad effects. In the case above, while the mistake involves opting for the option with the best outcome in terms of positive effects, Railton, or any objective consequentialist, would also consider in practical deliberation what is least likely to lead to bad effects. This does not mean that there is no truth of the matter as to which action is best given full information.

Jackson himself offers a view in which the right action is a function of what the agent actually believes and what the agent would desire given that he had the right set of values. So, what is right by the agent's own lights is what the agent would believe to be right given his own actual assessment of the probable outcomes and given that he had the right conception of value, the consequentialist conception of value. It is a function of what Jackson terms 'expected moral value', and in the above medicine case the *expected moral value* – due to moral safety considerations – is lower for drug X than for drug Y.

There are several things to note here. First, whatever the advantages of the decision-theoretic approach, it is not an alternative to objective consequentialism. For Jackson, it isn't the agent's *actual* psychology that determines the rightness of the action, since the agent needs to have the correct consequentialist value function – i.e. the right view of value, whatever that view is. Jackson's account is 'subjective' only in the sense that it ties rightness to the agent's actual beliefs.

Jackson also has a problem with negligent, or culpable, ignorance cases. The only way to deal with these cases is to idealize not just the agent's value function, but also the agent's beliefs – so the right action is understood relative to what the agent ought to believe. But Jackson wants to resist this, because it will not solve the action ownership problem, as it makes the standard too remote. He believes the culpable ignorance cases can be handled in the following way:

> Getting more information and then doing what has greatest moral utility has itself greatest moral utility provided the possible change in utility consequent on the new information when weighed by the probability of getting that new information is great enough to compensate for the effort and cost of getting the new information. Thus, working solely with a person's subjective probability function, with what he or she actually believes, we can distinguish plausibly between cases where more information ought to be obtained and where we may legitimately rest content with what we have.[41]

This doesn't fully solve the problem. There will be very many cases where the agent misjudges how much information is relevant, and makes the misjudgment sincerely, due to some other lack of information. A doctor may not order an extra test, thinking that a patient's cough is a cold when in fact it is pneumonia. And the doctor may be genuinely surprised later to find out the illness was much more serious than he thought. Assuming the extra test was called for as part of routine diagnostic procedures, we would, I think, view the doctor has having acted wrongly even if his actual subjective beliefs were – in his own mind – well founded.

Given the above arguments, we have at best a very strong *preliminary* case for the objective form of consequentialism that restricts the scope of consequences to what is foreseeable. In disagreement with Jackson, this involves idealizing the beliefs, since the agent may not actually foresee what is foreseeable. To fully develop this we need an account of 'foreseeable'. A good first run is to maintain that foreseeable effects are the ones a reasonably well-informed person at that time would be aware of or anticipate. This ties the rightness of the action to evidence that a reasonably well-informed person would be cognizant of.

This doesn't capture intuitions about cases where the agent doesn't know what a reasonable person would know, but through no fault of his own. Imagine a variation on Jackson's case. Suppose that a week before she treated John, there was a seminar at Jill's hospital on the very disease that John was suffering from. In the seminar new research was presented that demonstrated that John fell into a reference class for patients in which drug X would be a perfectly safe drug to use. Knowing this, of course, we would argue that she should prescribe drug X, because for patients like John there was virtually no risk of death and that drug would cure him. Jill failed to make it to the seminar, and thus ended up prescribing the wrong drug. She was not reasonably well informed. But our intuitions shift in Jill's favor if we discover that her colleague, Sam, who is normally extremely reliable and trustworthy, told her that she shouldn't bother going to the seminar that week – that it wouldn't be informative. In this case we don't view her failure to acquire relevant information as blameworthy, and this tends to reflect on how we view her subsequent action. Given what she knew, and what we think she should have known under the circumstances, she did do the right thing. Thus, when it comes to spelling out 'foreseeable' the more plausible characterization would involve relativizing it to what the reasonably attentive agent would know under the circumstances. Jill is attentive, and Sam mislead her, something that was not her fault.

All of these reasons are ones that have been given for preferring subjective over objective. But which version of objective is best? My claim is that (AO) is the correct account of 'right action' but that (FO) tracks much of our practice of praise and blame, though this is qualified later by noting that pragmatic factors relating to our interests in moral evaluation regulate praise and blame. (FO) provides its own *standard*, but it is a standard of praiseworthiness. This involves rejecting pure subjective consequentialism as the appropriate account of praise and blame. This argument will be made more thoroughly in the next chapter. The underlying thesis is that consequentialism is outcome-oriented, and procedures are evaluated in terms of their outcomes. What subjective consequentialists do is place priority in the procedure itself completely independently of the outcome, at least in principle.

A number of writers, Jackson included, note that there really is no mono-lithic sense of 'right'. The argument for giving an account of right action is to try to give an account that most accurately mirrors our views about evaluation. But there are many different senses of 'right' and 'ought' that have currency in our evaluative practices. For example, we can discuss the 'God's eye' view of right action, which holds that the right action just is the action that produces most good, impartially and cosmically considered. As noted earlier, though, this isn't something that has normal currency. Only God knows which actions are right. And then, of course, there is the other extreme where rightness is tied to what the agent actually believes and actually values, which results in all kinds of horrible actions being counted 'right' simply in view of the idiosyncratic and/or horribly mistaken views of the agent.

Because of this variation in usage, there are many writers who believe that 'right' and 'wrong' are just ambiguous between objective and subjec-tive senses.[42] Some also argue that while the objective sense serves some function for us, the subjective sense has primacy. This is because objective 'wrong' isn't really moral.[43] Consider the following case:

> (M) Mary is trying to decide whether or not she should make her chari-table donation to Oxfam or to her local community charity, Gofam, which provides counseling to troubled teenagers. She decides, after careful reflection, that she will give to Gofam. It is a local charity, and thus she will be in a better position, she thinks, to determine its success. She also feels that counseling teenagers is an important intervention that can do a great deal to promote their long-term happiness.

Let's suppose that the facts are as Mary thinks they are in (M). Counseling has long-term positive effects and it is good that people give to local charities (perhaps because, as in (M) they can gauge success better, perhaps because of the psychological connections, etc.). But suppose that there is more that Mary doesn't know, and could not reasonably be expected to know. Suppose that the director of Gofam is going through a difficult time. He is addicted to gambling and has run out of money. One night, two months after Mary has made her donation, he takes all of Gofam's money and leaves for Las Vegas. He squanders the money gambling. The money never makes it to the counseling centers that depend upon it. After reading of the scandal in the newspaper Mary may well decide that she did the 'wrong' thing by not giving the money to Oxfam, where she is fairly confident it would be well spent, even though she will never know exactly where. Subjective consequentialists argue that when Mary makes this judgment she is not judging that she did something morally wrong. She is simply making the judgment that it would have been better had she given the money to Oxfam. Similarly, it would have been better had the 1906 San Francisco earthquake never occurred, but that isn't a *moral* issue.

I don't think this is true, however. Mary is likely to feel very badly about not giving the money to Oxfam. She failed to succeed. Granted, it is not her fault that she failed to succeed, so she isn't blameworthy for the failure. Her action satisfies the praiseworthy standard even if it does not succeed. Mary *tried* to do what she thought was best, but she didn't. She failed. When one tries one tries to *do*. William Frankena has argued that whenever one has an obligation to try, that obligation is dependent on an obligation to do. His evidence is that, in circumstances where we know that we cannot bring about a certain state of affairs, and thus we have no obligation to bring it about, we also have no obligation to try to bring it about.[44] One subjective consequentialist, Elinor Mason, argues that really that's all we are obligated to do. We are only obligated to try to bring about the best results, not to actually bring them about. This is in part because trying is the only thing that is really within our power. But there are serious objections to this approach.

One major problem is the amoralist. If obligations are tryings, then for one to have an obligation to x one must have a belief that x is best and a desire to do it. Recall that the subjective consequentialist is arguing that people are only obligated to do what they are psychologically capable of doing. Amoralists lack such a desire. The subjective consequentialist here must simply bite the bullet. An amoralist does not have any moral obligations because the amoralist does not desire the morally best outcome and is not *capable* of trying. This is strongly counterintuitive. Ted Bundy had a moral obligation to refrain from killing women, even though he did not want to refrain from killing them. What an agent actually desires ought to have nothing to do with their obligations. Jackson recognized this in his account, and it is why his account is not fully subjective.

There are two senses of 'right', but the primary one is objective. The major positive argument for this comes in the last chapter. The subjective sense of 'right' nevertheless plays a significant role in our moral lives. This is because the subjective sense tracks appropriate praise and blame. In any given context, which sense is appropriate will be something that is sensitive to features of that context. Further, action evaluation is only one type of evaluation. We also evaluate motives, character traits, and intentions. In the next chapter I develop the objective account further by discussing global, contextual, consequentialism and the objective consequentialist's account of praise and blame.

Chapter summary

This chapter develops the distinction between subjective and objective forms of consequentialism, and argues in favor of the objective approach as a standard of act evaluation. This is in contrast to treating the subjective account of what it is to perform a right action as also providing an independent standard of right. The recent history of the debate is critically discussed.

Further reading

Peter Railton, "Alienation, Consequentialism, and the Demands of Morality," *Philosophy & Public Affairs* 13 (1984), 134–71.

Frank Jackson, "Decision-Theoretic Consequentialism and the Nearest and Dearest Objection," *Ethics* 101 (1991), 461–82.

Julia Driver, *Uneasy Virtue* (New York: Cambridge University Press, 2001), chs. 4 and 5.

Frances Howard-Snyder, "The Rejection of Objective Consequentialism," *Utilitas* 9 (1997), 241–8.

Elinor Mason, "Consequentialism and the Ought-Implies-Can Principle," *American Philosophical Quarterly* 40 (2003), 319–31.

6

CONSEQUENTIALISM AND PRACTICAL DELIBERATION

One fairly serious challenge to objective consequentialism, brought up earlier in this volume, is the criticism that it can't really say anything useful about practical deliberation. This view explicitly sets out a standard for *evaluation*, nothing more. Thus, the issue of how agents ought to think morally or approach moral problem-solving is left open, theoretically. It is an empirical issue as to what sorts of thought processes are the ones that tend to lead to better outcomes than others. It is an empirical issue as to what decision-procedures should be employed by moral agents to achieve the best overall results.

This was one of the factors behind Jackson's action-ownership problem discussed in the previous chapter. Jackson's main objection to objective consequentialism is that it privileges a sense of 'right action' that can't adequately account for the *action-guidance function* of moral theory. On Jackson's view, the derivative account the objective consequentialist gives of the subjective sense just isn't adequate and leads to numerous puzzles. I provided a limited response to this worry earlier, but the issue of whether an objective consequentialist can make recommendations about practical deliberation is interesting. Is there anything beyond just pointing out that what would count as the recommended decision-procedure is an empirical issue? Yes. It would be a trivial claim to point out that standards and decision-procedures are different – they are different. The objective consequentialist holds that the standard can be used to evaluate prospective decision-procedures. But a person who is employing the right sort of decision-procedure of course need not be aware of the standard that justifies the decision-procedure. So, in this sense, they are not being guided by the standard. Standards just don't work that way. What is interesting, though, is what we can say about action guidance in the case of persons who are committed to the standard. This chapter explores the issue of whether a commitment to the objective consequentialist standard of rightness can translate into providing practical guidance, and how this might plausibly work.

The general worry can be divided into two issues:

1   Given that (OC) specifies the standard for right action, what does this mean for an account of *reasons* we have to act morally (act according to the standard of *right*)?

2   What implications does (OC) have for how we go about *achieving* the standard, given we are committed to it?

Both of these issues figure into a well rounded account of practical deliberation: what reasons do we have for acting on the standard, and how do we go about reaching the standard?

Practical deliberation, as opposed to theoretical deliberation, is deliberation that governs *action*, where 'action' is understood fairly liberally. It is usually contrasted with theoretical deliberation, which is deliberation aimed at arriving at a warranted *belief*. The usual model for practical deliberation is instrumental: we deliberate, *practically*, about how we are to best go about achieving our ends. Our ends are set by what we desire. Thus, if I desire an ice cream cone and I know that I can most efficiently get an ice cream cone at the grocery store, then, given proper deliberation (given no contravening desires), I decide to go to the grocery store. This leads to my action of going to the grocery store. This is an example of someone being practically rational. The person's reason for going to the grocery store is to get ice cream, and the best way to do that is to go to the grocery store. If the same person decided to go to the hardware store instead of the grocery store, that would be practically irrational. It is a very poor place to acquire an ice cream cone. There is a very large debate about how 'subjective' practical rationality is. There is a shared assumption that moral norms are just a species of the practical, and while there is a sense in which this is true, it is true only if we distinguish different practical points of view that are irreducible to each other, and if we concede that making an evaluation is a kind of action. In the case of morality, the ends will be that which we ought to desire (under the circumstances). Jackson recognized the importance of at least this sort of idealization. Without it we would be forced to acknowledge that people act rightly even when they do truly horrific things, simply because they desire what is, objectively, bad, even if they don't recognize it as such. On this view, the reasons we have for acting rightly may be external – and this only makes sense if we view them as purely justifying reasons (as opposed to motivating ones). Moral reasons can be of two kinds: internal and external. Internal reasons are reasons an agent has for acting that are tied directly to her motivational set (i.e. what she actually wants or would want under conditions of ideal reflective consideration). External reasons are reasons that the agent has that are not tied directly to her motivational set.

A famous example comes from Bernard Williams, taken from Henry James' story in which Owen Wingrave's father "urges on him the necessity and importance of his joining the army, since all his male ancestors were soldiers, and family pride requires him to do the same. Owen Wingrave has no motivation to join the army at all, and all his desires lead in another direction: he hates everything about military life and what it means."[1] In this case, as Williams notes, Owen's father viewed Owen as having a reason to join the army, a reason provided by family tradition. But if Owen has such a reason, it is external since it is not tied to his motivational states. Even plumbing the deepest depths of Owen's desires we would find none satisfied by life in the army. Many believe that there are no such things as external reasons, since reasons by their very nature must motivate. But other philosophers note that justification and motivation are quite distinct, and there may be justifying external reasons that nevertheless lack motivational force for the individual who happens to have no desires to act in the ways the reasons specify. In this way one might say that a psychopath has a reason not to kill, even though he wants to kill and the killing would not interfere with any of this other projects. If this is the case, then the reason is external for the psychopath.

I believe that there are external reasons, but whatever one's view on this matter, it would be good for the consequentialist to explain why we have reason to act on the standard (whether or not it can be tied to our deep desires). Sidgwick's account of why we all have such reasons to adhere to the consequentialist standard draws on the view that the rational person is committed to the view that there is no morally relevant distinction between one's self and another. If each individual believes that his good is good not only *for him* but from the point of view of the Universe – as (*e.g.*) by saying that "nature designed him to seek his own happiness," – it then becomes relevant to point out to him that *his* happiness cannot be a more important part of Good, taken universally, than the equal happiness of any other person. And thus, starting with his own principle, he may be brought to accept Universal happiness or pleasure as that which is absolutely and without qualification Good or Desirable: as an end, therefore, to which the action of a reasonable agent as such ought to be directed.[2]

Thus, via rational reflection, the agent can come to see that he does have decisive moral reason to aim at the good of others as well as himself. Combined with the commitment to maximization, this makes the view very demanding. One can attempt to weaken the demands but at the risk of rendering the account too weak, in ways discussed earlier in the book. Lavishing resources on the 'near and dear' when others starve is not a morally permissible use of one's resources, either.

What of (2)? The analogy with the paradox of hedonism suggests that for the consequentialist, it is an empirical issue as to whether one ought to be committed to the consequentialist standard in assessing moral quality. Recall that Peter Railton suggested one way in which it seems plausible that a commitment that is not constantly kept before the mind is good-promoting. It is still the case that rightness depends on the effects of an action, though not the case that the agent must be thinking in those terms in order to actually perform the right action. Holding the standard to be regulative suggests that the standard can be used indirectly in assessing past policies and past actions in such a way as to have implications for future behavior. As such, it can figure into practical deliberation in certain ways.

For example, consider the case discussed in Chapter 5, in which Jill, a physician, lacks important information in treating a patient because she failed to attend a faculty development seminar. Upon reviewing her past actions she would come to realize that she could have had better patient outcomes had she gone to the seminar and acquired additional information. This, in turn, informs future decisions she makes about going to seminars on particular topics relevant to her medical practice. Her future deliberations will be informed by a review of successes and failures in past performance – and success or failure is determined by whether performance better matched actual good outcomes rather than outcomes she predicted to be good at the earlier time of action with the more limited epistemic resources.

In a similar manner, future advice from a friend or mentor is weighed according to past success. One thing we care about, of course, is whether our friend is sincerely advising us by giving us advice she genuinely thinks will prove best. But we also care about the accuracy of the advice – how close it gets to the actual best results relative to the options. This kind of retrospective assessment informs practical deliberation, and the assessment is performed with the objective standard as the standard against which one measures success.

Nevertheless, in spite of these observations, the objective standard has been attacked on the basis that if the actual consequences determine rightness then it is impossible for someone to be guided in her actions by such a standard for an entirely different reason as well. Human beings are epistemically limited. We can't know all the consequences of our actions. We can't know all the *likely* consequences of our actions, even. But a regulative ideal can guide perfectly well, *even* if it specifies a standard that is, for all practical purposes, impossible to achieve. The idea is that one simply does the best one can while making adjustments.

Suppose that Jane is in charge of constructing a new telescope for her university's observatory. She is told by her project engineer that the lenses for the telescope need to be perfectly smooth so as to eliminate light distortion. Even though it is impossible for her to create a lens that is perfectly smooth, she can nevertheless use that standard to guide her in grinding the lens, and then in evaluating the finished project. She simply does the best she can. Further, suppose that empirical research has shown that when someone is grinding lenses they get a better result if they don't actually think too carefully about their technique. Perhaps it helps, even, to imagine that one is doing something else entirely, such as sculpting or grading jewels. This would provide Jane a reason to not think too carefully about her technique, and to imagine she's doing something else. The reason is provided by the standard set for telescope lenses. The subjective standards employed in doing one's best to meet an objective standard are developed in the service of meeting that standard. Subjective standards are very important to a full-fledged theory of moral evaluation, but they are not primary. Recall in the previous chapter the discussion of the standard for an action's praiseworthiness.

Consider another analogy. It is often claimed that belief aims at truth. We evaluate the belief in part on the basis of whether it is true or false. Yet if we have very exacting standards for what it is for a belief to be true, then we may never in actuality be able to meet that standard. Indeed, for all practical purposes all of us fail to meet the standard. None of us is such that all of our beliefs are true. It does not follow from this that the standard is thereby to be rejected. A commitment to such a standard can still guide. Thus, the objective standard provides material for guiding our actions as well as cultivating dispositions that promote the good.

It is also possible to reject the question and simply hold that the function of moral theory is to provide a criterion for evaluation, and it needn't say anything about practical deliberation. In effect, this would be to give priority to the metaphysical issue, the issue of articulating just what it is that makes an action 'right', over the epistemological issue of how we go about determining, or figuring out, what the right action is. It may be that these two are related in that one goes about determining the right action through a simple, straightforward application of the criterion. Indeed, this will certainly often be the case, though I've noted throughout this book cases in which this simple model breaks down. Often people do not have a clear idea of the reasons they are responding to in acting morally, and yet – if we take them to actually be responding to a particular reason that, in the given context, is the reason that they *ought* to be responding to so as to promote the good – then we do view them as acting in a praiseworthy way. This was the point behind the Le Chambon case discussed earlier. What makes the villagers' actions right is that they saved children from being murdered, and they did so out of sympathy for the children, to prevent their suffering. The reasons cited might be all sorts of *other* things having to do with Huguenot religious beliefs, and so forth, but the religious beliefs in and of themselves do not morally justify – it is the prevention of the suffering that morally justifies. To insist on conscious adherence to a deliberative process in which the correct criterion is explicitly applied flies in the face of our practice. The standard analogy is with grammar. A person can speak English perfectly well without consciously applying the rules of good grammar.

But the objective consequentialist can still have something to say about practical deliberation in order to supplement the account of evaluation. Recall that on the objective view the right action is the one that maximizes the good, among the relevant options. What are the relevant options? They have to be options that are open to the agent at the time of action. Thus, they must consist of actions that are possible for the agent to perform and possible for the agent to choose. If we believe that these options must be open to deliberation on the part of the agent, then deliberation is a feature of the account. Note that the deliberation in question *can* still be idealized, as discussed earlier in the book. But it is more in keeping with objective consequentialism to restrict the scope of relevant alternatives to those actions that are possible for the agent to perform at the time of action.

Why include the options clause? Suppose that Mary sees that someone on the other side of the lake where she is swimming is drowning, but there is no way for her to get to the other side of the lake to help the person. 'Getting to the other side of the lake' is not an option for her. She lacks the requisite physical capabilities. Subjective consequentialists, in effect, are very restrictive on the issue of options. On their view the agent must be aware of her options as options. The objective consequentialist denies this. But there can still be an objective fact of the matter about what the agent's options *are* beyond what is simply logically and physically possible for the agent.

There are different ways in which an action can be called 'right', though the guiding norm is that of production of actual good. However, I also argued that 'praiseworthy' is orthogonal to this. And, on my view, it tracks the use of 'right' that corresponds to production of foreseeable good. This is compatible with an objective standard, recall, since the standard of praiseworthiness is justified by appeal to the objective standard. The aim of moral action is success. We admire those who act with the aim of succeeding. There are two senses of 'right', though the primary sense is objective. While foreseeable is not the same as 'foreseen', it often, in actual practice, corresponds to foreseen. And this raises the issue of what sorts of options agents ought to be considering when they do find themselves in a position of thinking in terms of deciding on the basis of consequences. Consider, for example, someone who wants to be a good consequentialist moral agent and who would like to live her life in the best way possible along consequentialist lines. What should be ruled in or out for her in the area of options? Because the view that I favor (and that seems more in keeping with the spirit of the objective approach) is that the third-person evaluative viewpoint has priority, the agent should try to consider the advice she would be given by a third party. This is just a heuristic, though. The reason to consider how an advisor would advise one is that there is a difference between an option that one *can* take and an option that one predicts quite reliably one *will* take.

For example, a classic problem in this regard has to do with whether agents should be sensitive to their own predictions of how they will in fact act in the future, or consider only how they *could* act in the future. This debate is one of interest to any theory of practical deliberation. The consequentialist holds that the right action is the one that maximizes the good amongst the range of relevant alternatives. Deciding what is to count as a 'relevant alternative' is of interest, then, to understanding the full account. Actualists hold that the best option is understood relative to what the agent likely will do, whereas the possibilists hold that the best option is understood relative to what the agent could reasonably do. This can be articulated both objectively and subjectively. Here, however, we focus on the role of this consideration in practical deliberation. If one is a consequentialist, and if one does think that the objective standard is the right one, how should one go about making one's decisions? That is, how should one think on this issue if one is concerned to act in a blameless or at least less blameworthy way? If one is committed to objective consequentialism as a standard, then one interesting question has to do with whether one should be an actualist or a possibilist in one's actual reasoning. Recall this issue came up earlier, in Chapter 3.

Frank Jackson and Robert Pargetter put the basic distinction between actualism and possibilism the following way:

> By *Actualism* we will mean the view that the values that should figure in determining which option is the best and so ought to be done out of a set of options are the values of what *would* be the case were the agent to adopt or carry out the option, where what would be the case includes of course what the agent would simultaneously or subsequently in fact do: the (relevant) value of an option is the value of what would in fact be the case were the agent to perform it. We will call the alternative view that it is only necessary to attend to what is possible for the agent, *Possibilism*.[3]

This is of interest to the consequentialist because she will be concerned to figure out what goes into deciding the best option given certain considerations, such as her views about what will happen in the future as opposed to what could happen in the future. To illustrate the distinction between these two positions, Jackson and Pargetter ask us to consider the case of a procrastinator who is asked to write a book review. 'Procrastinate' knows that, ideally, the best thing for him to do is to say "yes" and write the review on time; however, he also knows that he procrastinates, and will not write the review on time, in which case the best thing is to say "no." The question is, what is the right thing for him to do, or what ought he to do? The actualist will argue that he should say "no," but on the possibilist position he ought to say "yes." The actualist position is the one advocated by Jackson and Pargetter. There is a good deal of intuitive support for the view – denying it would seem to endorse the worse outcome.[4]

In the above case, then, the actualist says "no" to the book review because the expected utility of saying "yes," given what he knows about himself, and what he will actually do or what will actually happen, is less than the expected utility of saying "no." The actual outcome of saying "no" then is most likely better (that is, is *expected* by the agent to be better). In respect to the restriction of options for the agent to consider, I agree with Jackson that actualism is the correct account. My agreement is based on the view that this gives us a smooth transition between the third-person evaluative perspective and the factors most likely to succeed in consequentialist practical deliberation. One can view the actualism, then, as tying into the account of praise and blame offered by the theory. Again, the objective consequentialist standard is distinct from this issue. The connection is simply that the standard allows us to evaluate approaches to practical deliberation as better or worse. If the better outcomes come from an actualist approach then a person committed to consequentialism, given reasonable empirical assumptions, ought to opt for the actualist approach.

Again, it would seem that actualism has a good deal of intuitive support, because the alternative seems to endorse the worse outcome. However, a number of philosophers disagree with the actualist position. Michael Zimmerman, for example, has argued in favor of possibilism, using the following case to generate possibilist intuitions:

> Alf has been invited to attend a wedding. The bride-to-be, Brenda, is a former girlfriend of his; it was she who did the dumping. Everyone, including Alf in his better moments, recognizes that Brenda was quite right to end the relationship; they were not well suited to one another, and the prospects were bleak. Her present situation is very different; she and her fiancé, Charles, sparkle in one another's company, spreading joy wherever they go. This irks Alf no end, and he tends to behave badly (though not murderously) whenever he sees them together. He ought not to misbehave, of course, and he knows this; he could quite easily resist the temptation to do so, but so far he hasn't. The wedding will be an opportunity for him to put this sort of boorishness behind him, to grow up and move on. The best thing for him to do would be to accept the invitation, show up on the day in question, and behave himself. The worst thing would be to show up and misbehave; better would be to decline the invitation and not show up at all.[5]

The actualist would maintain that he ought to decline the invitation, whereas the possibilist would hold he should accept it. Zimmerman's intuitions are that the possibilist is correct in this case. I don't share those intuitions, but Zimmerman's case rests on the view that the actualist allows people to get off the hook, morally, by appealing to their deficiencies. Further, he (as well as many other writers) notes that actualism seems to be committed to the denial of: if S ought to do both A and B, then S ought to do A and S ought to do B. This he thinks is absurd. Suppose that Alf agrees that the best thing for him to do is to (1) accept the invitation, (2) go to the party, and (3) behave himself. He agrees that he ought to do *all three*. Yet, if he accepts the actualist position, he is also saying that he ought not to accept the invitation in the first place. This seems incoherent to Zimmerman.

This does seem odd. I don't think this oddity survives reflection, though. It will not work in any case where the goodness of B *depends on* A. S ought to do B, given A. Note that in combination with the decision-theoretic approach the picture is something like this: the best outcome is the one where Alf shows up at the wedding and behaves himself, just as when one is in Las Vegas the best outcome is the one where one gambles and wins. However, the expected utility of the 'best' outcome under ideal circumstances is pretty low in the gambling case, and if, similarly, it is pretty low in the wedding case then Alf ought not to go to the wedding since he is very likely not to achieve the 'best outcome under ideal circumstances'. And this isn't simply a matter of assigning low probabilities to acting well. Even if the probability is relatively high that Alf will act well, it may still be the case he ought not accept if a failure to act well would be very bad. That's because the expected utility would be low enough to make acceptance a bad idea.

Let's consider two different comparisons:

1   Compare the cases where I factor in what I can expect to actually *happen*. For example, I plan on throwing a party and it would be best if I could throw it in my beautiful garden on a sunny day. However, this would be worst in the event of a rainstorm – under those circumstances it would be far better to have the party inside. If I know it will rain, then, should I not arrange for the party inside (even though the best is having it outside under sunny skies)? Clearly, yes. However, possibilists will of course say this sort of calculation is entirely different from the sort they are concerned with, as in the Procrastinate case. They will argue that it may be fine to calculate the 'behavior' of objects, and the occurrence of certain events, but I cannot treat myself as an object or event – after all, I can control my behavior. I am an agent, not an object.[6]

But then consider the second comparison:

2   Compare this with cases where the goodness depends on what others do. Sally ought to give 2 percent of her income to Oxfam, *given* everyone else does. If few other people do, she ought to give 10 percent of her income to Oxfam. The rightness of giving the 2 percent depends upon what others are doing or going to do, and of course, I can't treat others as mere objects in my calculations either, can I? Well, the possibilist will respond that to the extent that you don't have appropriate control over them, they are relevantly like events. The point, they will say, is that you are an agent, and you certainly have control over what you will do (with the appropriate caveats). However, this line of argument can be countered by a factor Jackson and Pargetter bring out in support of their claim: Consider the sort of advice that ought to be given to Procrastinate. Given that you know he is not going to write the review on time, you ought to *advise* him not to accept the invitation to write it, instead to say "no." Given that you ought to advise him to say "no" then it follows that he ought to say "no."

But this line of argument has been attacked. For example, Erik Carlson presents the following scenario. Suppose we have three options, *a*, *b*, *c*: *a* is the best, *b* second-best, *c* the worst. Suppose also that if you give someone any advice other than the advice to do *b*, he will instead to *c*. The possibilist would argue that he still ought to do *a*, though you ought to tell him to do *b*. To deny this is simply to beg the question against the possibilist.[7]

In a way these observations offer a way to slip agent-relativity into the account. The possibilist wants us to view the moral agent making his own decision as quite different from the agent advising others, or deciding what to do on the basis of how he thinks others will act. However, on my view this raises an interesting theoretical issue: it looks as if we should, in effect, on the possibilist view, be actualists of a sort when it comes to considering other events and the behavior of others, and possibilist when it comes to our own behavior. After all, this is what would allow Carlson's argument against Jackson and Pargetter to have any force. The agent ought to do *a*, nevertheless he should be advised to do *b*. We are asked, then, to be realistic when it comes to factoring in what others do, or what other things happen, into our calculations; but not to do this when it comes to our own behavior, over which we have some control. One way to view the divide is to note that possibilism seems to capture the perspective of the agent choosing and actualism the perspective of the observer advising. If this is right, then actualism does seem poorly suited to combination with the subjective view, which is supposed to privilege the perspective of the deliberating agent, the agent making the choice, in determinations of right. There's no logical incompatibility. Jackson would simply note that the agent considers what she believes she will do in determinations of rightness. But this just exacerbates the problems that the possibilist raises for the *actualist* view. Actualism with the subjective view of right really does seem to let the agent off the hook.

There is a good deal of intuitive support for the possibilist view, too, provided by even more extreme cases: for example, suppose that Roberta needs money and is thinking of robbing a bank. Roberta ought not to rob the bank at all, but if she does she ought not use a gun that could harm innocent persons, or even lead to such persons' death. If Roberta decides that she is just too weak and will rob the bank anyway (though she won't use a gun) – well, then the actualist seems committed to the view that robbing the bank (albeit without a gun) is what she ought to do. This seems to allow way too much consideration for an agent's weaknesses and imperfections.[8] My position will reject this implication while admitting that given that she is going to rob a bank she ought not to use a gun. That is because I will be arguing for a separation between 'right' and 'ought'. Further, the intuitive implausibility of that judgment can be mitigated by building the relevant contrasts into the judgment. "The right thing for Roberta to do is rob the bank without a gun" does seem outrageous. "The right thing for Roberta to do is rob the bank without a gun, *rather than* rob the bank with a gun" is far less counterintuitive. If she is going to rob the bank, it just seems true.

Consider Sally's case again. Sally ought to give 2 percent of her income to Oxfam, given everyone else does. If few other people do give to Oxfam, she ought to give 10 percent of her income to Oxfam. The rightness of giving the 2 percent depends upon what *others* are doing or going to do. If they aren't going to give (though they ought to) the right thing for her to do is give 10 percent. That's the best she can do. She ought to give 10 percent given that she realizes that others will not be giving their fair share – the share that they could reasonably give. Doesn't it make sense, then, to suppose that whether the spurned boyfriend ought to go to the wedding depends upon what he *will* do?

As in handling Jackson's advice argument, a possibilist, however, might note that there is a crucial difference between first- and third-person perspectives, the perspective of the agent as opposed to the observer. However, both of these standards are relevant only to the epistemological issue of what criterion to use in determining how best to proceed. Given that he will misbehave if he goes, he ought not to go to the wedding, and it would be the wrong thing for him to do so. This is just a reminder that this issue needs to be separated from the issue of understanding what is the right action, or, rather, what 'right action' means. Under the circumstances as described, the right thing for the spurned boyfriend to do is not go to the wedding rather than to go and act foolishly. In determining what he *ought* to do he should again try to think in terms of what he believes will (or is likely to) happen – if he believes he will misbehave, that's an important reason not to go. The actualist decision-procedure simply incorporates more realism into the moral decision-making process.

'Best' is central to our understanding of 'right'. The right thing will be the best thing among available options. But what someone ought to do is (quite likely) what she believes has the best payoff relative to what she believes, sincerely, will happen. It is this latter sense of 'ought' which invites praise and blame. But the former sense is, nevertheless, instructive. Awareness of the best option serves *some* guiding function even if one is not aiming for the best. It is a mistake to think that the only way one is guided by some end is through aiming at the end. Here is just one of many possible cases to illustrate this: Maria realizes that, though she did fairly well by deciding to major in communication, the best choice for her would have actually been psychology. She wishes now that she had decided to major in psychology. This motivates her to make further career choices sensitive to that preference. Though it is too late to redo her major, she can still seek employment in areas more amenable to her interest in psychology.

This approach has the advantage of making sense of 'contrary-to-duty' imperatives. These are imperatives of the form "Don't do x, but if you do x, don't also do y." Remember the case of Roberta, a case that posed a major intuitive difficulty for the actualist approach? Well, this hybrid approach would hold that it would be wrong for Roberta to steal, which would not be the right thing for her to do. However, given that she is going to steal, she ought to follow a decision-procedure that minimizes harm. Thus, she ought not to use a gun, given that she is going to steal. In *this context*, it makes sense to say "She ought not to use a gun." But, given my account, this does not make stealing the right thing for her to do even if she does not use a gun. Thus, I believe this hybrid approach can avoid Zimmerman's problem, which holds that it lets the moral agent off the hook. It doesn't. It just offers a nuanced evaluation. The judgement of what one ought to do in the sense of what is praiseworthy, as well as what it is 'right' for one to do, are understood relative to contrasts.

Chapter summary

If one is committed to objective consequentialism, is there anything that can plausibly be said about how one ought to go about deciding what to do, apart from simply noting that what counts as a good decision-procedure is empirical? This chapter argues "yes," given that one makes some pretty intuitive empirical assumptions. The central debate of the chapter involves the distinction between actualism and possibilism. Actualists hold that in deciding what to do we consider what we believe is likely to actually happen – including what we believe about ourselves, what we believe we ourselves are likely to do. Possibilists, on the other hand, hold that in deciding what to do we consider what we think the best option is amongst the ones that we can do, not amongst the ones that we think we will in fact perform. In this chapter I argue in favor of actualism by noting that it is more in keeping with objective consequentialism's focus on actual outcomes.

Further reading

Holly Smith, "Culpable Ignorance," *Philosophical Review* 92 (1983), 543–71.

Erik Carlson, "Consequentialism, Alternatives, and Actualism," *Philosophical Studies* 96 (1999), 253–68.

Michael Zimmerman, *Living with Uncertainty* (New York: Cambridge University Press, 2008).

Douglas Portmore, *Commonsense Consequentialism* (New York: Oxford University Press, 2011), ch. 7.

Jacob Ross, "Actualism, Possibilism, and Beyond," in *Oxford Studies in Normative Ethics*, vol. 2, ed. Mark Timmons (New York: Oxford University Press, forthcoming).

7

GLOBAL CONSEQUENTIALISM

Bernard Williams echoed a view popular to many in the 1980s when he wrote in his famous exchange with J. J. C. Smart that "the simple-mind-edness of utilitarianism disqualifies it totally."[1] What did Williams mean by simple-minded? This criticism is actually multi-faceted. Williams was making a point, often echoed by later virtue ethicists, that insofar as the theory focuses on right action, it is ignoring a great deal of the nuance of moral evaluation. Of course, consequentialism may be thought to share this flaw with many other theories, but the other feature of the view that is simple-minded is its seeming commitment to there being one right answer about right action, at least in the vast majority of cases. But these criticisms are not at all deep. They simply point to a deficiency in the consequentialist's public relations division. Even if, historically, the main focus of the theory has been on act evaluation, the focus on articulating a theory of right action, with little attention paid to other modes of moral evaluation, this indicates nothing essential about the theory at all. Ethics is practical, and as practical the natural focus will be on act evaluation. However, insofar as other factors are relevant to good-promotion, those factors will also be evaluable under the consequentialist standard.

As we have seen, writers such as Derek Parfit and Peter Railton took steps to remedy the perceived deficit. Even more recently attention has been paid to expanding the consequentialist standard well beyond act evaluation.

One reason why there has been a renewed interest in character in conse-quentialism has to do with the consideration that many counterintuitive aspects of consequentialism can be mitigated by noting that moral evaluation is nuanced. But it is also just *true* that character is evaluable along consequentialist lines. It isn't just actions and rules that can be evaluated morally. Motives, intentions, character traits – these are all aspects of a person that are subject to evaluation when someone acts, or even when we have access to their inner states independent of their *actions* (as we often do with fictional characters, for example). Further, there is more to evaluation than 'rightness'. The use of virtue terms, or aretaic terms as opposed to deontic ones, constitutes a form of moral evaluation. When Maria claims that Sarah is a generous person she is attributing a virtue to her, she is praising her, and that form of evaluation can also be given a consequentialist analysis. I've argued elsewhere that nuanced evaluations which note the distinction between act evaluation and character evaluation give us a better sense of moral ambiguity.[2] Suppose that Alice has generously given her cousin some money, thinking to help him out financially, though her cousin ends up misspending the money. One could hold that she did the wrong thing in helping him out, even though it was compassionate, and, in that sense, morally good. In situations where moral ambiguity arises we have competing parameters of evaluation. On my view, global consequentialism holds that all features of agency are subject to moral evaluation so can best diagnose this ambiguity.

Roughly speaking, global consequentialism is the view that the moral quality of any *evaluand* is determined by its consequences. Derek Parfit refers to this approach as 'C' and as he notes, the central aim of C is:

> (C1) There is one ultimate moral aim: that outcomes be as good as possible. C applies to everything.[3]

Philip Pettit and Michael Smith articulate the notion in the following way:

> Global consequentialism identifies the right *x*, for any *x* in the category of evaluands – be the evaluands acts, motives, rules, or whatever – as the best *x*, where the best *x*, in turn, is that which maximizes value.[4]

This is not general enough. Moral quality may take forms other than 'rightness', though 'rightness' is the focus of most consequentialist theories of evaluation. Global consequentialism is understood in contrast to local consequentialism. Local consequentialism privileges one sort of evaluand, such as actions, in the case of local act-consequentialism. As Pettit and Slote point out, the local version of act-consequentialism holds that the right action maximizes value, and that other evaluands are understood relative to their production of such actions. Rules are deemed 'right' if they produce right action. But global consequentialism does not privilege any evaluand. The right rule to use is the rule that itself produces more value, and so forth with actions, motives, desires.

Note that global consequentialism is quite distinct from indirect forms of consequentialism that focus on, for example, rules, and then define right action or right motive relative to the right rules. The standard version of rule-utilitarianism, for example, is incompatible with global consequentialism since it privileges, still, act evaluation though the act evaluation is understood relative to rules. For global consequentialism, rather, the right motive, or motive set; the right desire; the right intention; the right rule; the right action are all on an evaluative par. This allows for a very rich evaluative landscape.

The form I would like to argue for is the more general form:

(GG) The *moral quality* of *x* is determined solely by the consequences of *x*, where *x* is understood as a feature of agency or relevant to agency.

This does not commit one to another sort of privileging — that is, privileging 'right' as the mode of evaluation. We evaluate using virtue terms, for example, or using expressions such as 'admirable' that can't be captured by 'right'. The more general form of global consequentialism takes this into account, holding that a trait that is a virtue, for example, is one whose moral quality is understood in terms of its production of good effects.

In *Uneasy Virtue*, I developed a consequentialist account of moral virtue that defined moral virtue as a character trait that leads, overall and systematically, to good effects. This account conforms to (GG) but not to the original Parfit definition since it says, as it stands, nothing about the *rightness* of the character trait. But (GG) is simply a more general understanding of what Parfit originally had in mind, and what other writers have followed up on.

Why limit moral evaluation to agency (or features involved with agency such as intentions, motives, etc.)? Here again one appeals to the practical nature of ethics. We often do speak of 'the right hammer' or 'the right eye color' but when 'right' is being used in its distinctively moral sense the context will always be one in which the consideration of rightness matters for choice. Consider the following: Melissa and her friends have been caught up in a tornado emergency in their town and stranded atop an unstable building. Suppose that Melissa needs to hammer a ladder into place in order to facilitate the survival of herself and her friends, by securing a means of escape before the building collapses. She has a range of hammers to choose from. The right hammer will be the one that works best and will do a good job of fixing the ladder. The right hammer is the one that Melissa needs to use in order to promote the good, it is the one that she ought to choose. There is no 'right' hammer in absence of the choice situation. What this indicates to me is that 'right hammer' is shorthand for 'the hammer it would be right for Melissa to select for this job'; and, thus, the evaluand is the selection itself. If Melissa fails to choose that hammer then she has failed morally.[5]

Simple action isn't the only morally significant practical consideration or choice we face. We are also concerned with living a morally good life. The standard for this is in one sense maximizing – of course, a rational person would like to live the overall best life possible. But living such a life will involve developing traits that themselves are not thought of as maximizing. They are just part of the maximally good life; traits that we think of as virtues such as generosity and fairness. These traits are also differentiated by the consequentialist criterion.[6] A virtue is a trait that *systematically* produces good effects. It is not picked out by any particular psychological state, such as good intentions or motives. But this observation about the rightness of action and the virtue status of character traits doesn't rest on a rejection of the moral significance of psychological states such as motives and intention. These themselves can be evaluated along consequentialist lines. What makes a motive good? It is the sort of motive associated with production of good effects. If a type of motive does not produce good effects systematically, it is not good.

Writers such as Derek Parfit, Michael Smith, and Philip Pettit have noted that the answers to questions about what good an action does as opposed to what good a desire does, or a motive, or a life, are all independent:

> Notwithstanding the intimate connection between the desires people have and the acts that those desires produce, it therefore follows that, since their desires can have effects independently of these acts ... consequentialism may tell people to perform certain acts, but also tell them to have desires which are quite different from those that they would have if they were to perform all of those acts.[7]

This separation allows us to make judgments in greater detail. Michael Smith notes that *global* big 'C' consequentialism allows us to give a powerful response to the 'nearest and dearest' objection. Recall from discussion in an earlier chapter that big 'C' consequentialism is committed to *neutral* value. Even though it is committed to there being only neutral value, the global big 'C' consequentialist can well hold that we ought to maximize neutral value, and thus the right action for any agent is the one that maximizes the good, impartially considered. However, it is also able to note that having the sort of character that promotes neutral value can militate against acting in neutral terms in specific cases. Thus, it is true that Mary should send her $100 to Oxfam rather than buy her daughter a new radio, if what we are considering is the evaluation of her action. However, it does not follow from this that she should be the sort of person who would send her money to Oxfam rather than buy things that would make her children happier.

> [S]ince the consequences of our actions and our character are non-identical, no conclusion about the character we ought to have, or the life we ought to lead, can be drawn from ... consequentialism's answer to the question 'Which actions ought we to perform?'[8]

Global consequentialism provides the resources necessary for explaining *evaluative ambivalence*. Evaluative ambivalence refers to the phenomenon of an evaluator being torn between descriptions of an action as right or wrong, or good or bad. There are numerous examples of people acting wrongly, even though they've tried to act rightly, or even though they exhibit good dispositions and motives. Alice wants to help her aunt, and genuinely cares about her aunt, but her well-intentioned insistence that her aunt get enough exercise ends up leaving her aunt worse off with a broken leg. She should not have been insistent, that was wrong, but her motives and intentions were good ones. If we follow the definition set out by Pettit and Smith, then, one could say she didn't do the right thing, or have the right motive, either, since the results were so bad. But this seems rather odd to me. She did have the right motive, even though she performed the wrong act. But this doesn't cut against the broader global consequentialism that I favor. The action was wrong, because it resulted in overall bad effects, but the motive was a morally good motive because motives aimed at helping others generally succeed and have good effects. The motive is a morally good motive, because of the effects associated with that kind of motive. We (generally speaking) like people to have good motives and refrain from having bad ones, so we encourage that via praise and blame that tracks these evaluations.

Some criticize global consequentialism because they believe that the advice it gives is inconsistent.[9] One example is the following, taken from Parfit:

> Clare could either give her child some benefit, or give much greater bene-
> fits to some unfortunate stranger. Because she loves her child, she benefits
> him rather than the stranger.[10]

This is an example of what Parfit terms 'blameless wrongdoing'. Clare should have given the benefit to the stranger, who would have gained more. That was the right thing for her to do. However, the love that motivated her action in giving the benefit to her child is good, too, on consequentialist grounds, because if she didn't love her child, things would be much worse. The disposition to love her child, then, is the right one to have. So, Clare ought to give to the stranger, but her disposition, which she also ought to have, pushes her to give to her child instead. This is the contradiction that concerns Bart Streumer, since he holds that if a person ought to do A and ought also to do B, then the person ought to do (A&B).[11] But Clare cannot both love her child and help the stranger. Getting rid of agglomeration is one way to solve the problem.[12] However, the problem doesn't arise for the more general form of global consequentialism. Clare can love her child and help the stranger, though she cannot both act on loving her child in that particular context and help the stranger. Her disposition is morally good, though it leads to a suboptimal motive in that particular instance, which in turn leads her to perform the wrong action. But she, as an agent, is still praiseworthy, or at least not blameworthy. Streumer's criticism would miss the mark because 'ought to' is relative to the evaluand. Clare ought to be a good mother as well as promote the good, impartially considered. There will be many situations in which these 'oughts' conflict, but because the oughts are relative to different considerations, there is no real inconsistency. There is simply a practical dilemma, and we are all familiar with practical dilemmas.

However, if one is a global consequentialist, is there some fact of the matter about what one ought, *all* things considered, to do? Note that this does not commit one to a view that we must give up the overridingness of moral reasons. The moral reasons are the same, in that the moral reasons are provided by the moral standard – that of promoting the good. Instead, there are different ways one promotes the good, through action directly, being disposed to act a certain way, being motivated a certain way, and so on. In the ambivalence cases discussed earlier, these ways conflict. In conflict cases, does right action trump good motive, or not?

How the global consequentialist responds to this will depend on the extent to which our subsequent actions can be insulated from the rejection of our morally good dispositions and motives. Consider the following case, presented by Robert Adams, which is supposed to illustrate wrong action from a good motive:

> Jack is a lover of art who is visiting the cathedral at Chartres for the first time. He is greatly excited by it, enjoying it enormously ... He is so excited that he is spending much more time at Chartres than he had planned. ... In fact, he is spending too much time there, from a utilitarian point of view. ... On the whole, he will count the day well spent, but some of the time spent in the cathedral will not produce as much utility as would have been produced by departing that much earlier.[13]

Jack is acting wrongly, but from a really good motivational set. He has praiseworthy motives that induce him to stay longer than he really ought at the cathedral. What ought Jack to do?

Jack ought to leave earlier. Again, global consequentialism is not a form of indirect consequentialism, which advocates a course of action based on the effects of a rule, a disposition, or a certain motivational set. The right action just will be the action that produces the best outcome. That's what Jack ought to do, the action that produces the best outcome. But this is separate from the issue of what sort of dispositions Jack ought to have.

This leaves open the possibility that one ought not to be the sort of person who always performs the right action. And this renders an account of moral perfection much more complicated. There has been some debate about whether one ought to try to be morally perfect. There is some intuitive support that seeking moral perfection is a worthy and admirable goal. In his *Autobiography*, Benjamin Franklin discusses his failed attempts to cultivate perfection.

> I conceiv'd the bold and arduous project of arriving at moral perfection. I wish'd to live without committing any fault at any time; I would conquer all that either natural inclination, custom, or company might lead me into. As I knew, or thought I knew, what was right and wrong, I did not see

why I might not always do the one and avoid the other. But I soon found I had undertaken a task of more difficulty than I had imagined. While my care was employ'd in guarding against one fault, I was often surprised by another; habit took the advantage of inattention; inclination was sometimes too strong for reason.[14]

Franklin laments the difficulty of actually achieving moral perfection, though still considers it something to strive for. As his experience indicates, moral perfection tends to be taken as perfection in action. Thus, one plausible suggestion is that moral perfection is the following:

(MP) An agent is morally perfect iff the agent always does what is right and never does what is wrong.[15]

However, if one accepts a global theory of moral evaluation, then (MP) is clearly too narrow an account of moral perfection. To be morally perfect one also has to have the best character. And, if the above observation about Jack is correct, then one cannot both have the best character and satisfy (MP). This doesn't show that moral perfection is not conceptually possible. It simply shows that an account of moral perfection would have to consider what the *possibilities* are for any given agent, so would have to be more nuanced than the ones suggested in the literature so far. For Jack to display perfection in action, in the case as described, he would have to exhibit an inferior motivational structure. We think he is well motivated in being swept up in the glories of Chartres, though recognizing that overstaying the visit is a failure as well.

One assumption that should be challenged, for example, is that moral perfection somehow involves epistemic perfection. This is simply not true. In earlier works I have argued for the existence of a class of moral virtues that involve epistemic defect of some sort. A virtue such as modesty may involve the agent making an error – albeit a relatively small error – about his or her accomplishments.[16] But further, on the view I argue for in this book, the ultimate standard is production of good. We can grant that the more we know the better we are, in general, at actually achieving the good – but this is an empirical issue. And even if it holds in general, it does not hold across the board. As the modesty case shows, acting modestly involves a lack of knowledge that is needed for the agent to exhibit the virtue. Other examples involve engaging in self-deception in order to achieve some greater good. For example, perhaps, in order to be a nurturing parent, one needs to have a slightly inflated view of one's children's accomplishments and abilities – in order to keep pushing them, however slightly, in the right direction. Lacking a fully accurate view is needed to enable motivation to achieve the best outcome. In this case, one is discussing lack of knowledge with respect to others; Benjamin Franklin believed that his mistaken view that he could acquire moral perfection was nevertheless useful because it helped him to push himself to become a much better person. For these reasons we need to resist the view that it must be the case that more knowledge always makes for better outcomes.

Consequentialism in its global form is a theory of moral evaluation that provides one with the resources for the kind of nuanced moral evaluations that reflect our best moral practices. It also provides us with a criterion that can be used to guide our actions on the basis of adopting rules, cultivating dispositions, and encouraging motives that – to the best of our knowledge – lead to good outcomes in the actual world. It answers the challenges made in the last half century against utilitarianism by appealing to finer-grained moral evaluations. I am sure not all will agree, but this theory of moral evaluation is the best on offer.

Chapter summary

In this chapter a general form of objective global consequentialism is presented. On this view, moral quality of intentions, character traits, motives, and so forth, as well as actions, are evaluated on the basis of objective consequentialist standards. The advantages of the approach are discussed, particularly its ability to account for cases of normative ambivalence, in which a person may feel that a particular action is really the right action, and yet also feel that there is something not quite right about it. This can be diagnosed as a case in which act evaluation is in divergence from the evaluation of some other feature of agency, such as the person's character.

Further reading

Philip Pettit and Michael Smith, "Global Consequentialism," in *Morality, Rules, and Consequences*, ed. Brad Hooker, Elinor Mason, and Dale Miller (Lanham, MD: Rowman & Littlefield, 2000), 121–33.

Bart Streumer, "Can Consequentialism Cover Everything?" *Utilitas* 15 (2003), 237–47.

GLOSSARY

action-ownership problem   Objective consequentialists are committed to the view that the rightness of an action is determined by its consequences, rather than, for example, what the agent expects to be the consequences. As such, the agent's psychology is irrelevant to the action's rightness, and this is taken to raise the action-ownership problem: in what sense does the objective consequentialist believe that agents 'own' their own actions in the sense of being *morally responsible for* their own actions? It seems problematic to hold a person responsible for something she did not anticipate happening as a result of her action.

actualism (with respect to relevant options)   The view that the agent ought to consider what she thinks she will do rather than what she could do in deciding between options.

alienation in morality   A perceived problem in which an agent's values, and the actual justification for her actions, come apart.

average consequentialism   The view that we ought to maximize average utility.

consequentialism   The view that the moral quality of a feature of agency is determined completely by its consequences, relative to relevant alternatives.

Act-consequentialism: the right action is the action that maximizes the good, amongst the options open to the agent performing the action.

Rule-consequentialism: the right action is the action that is performed in accordance with a set of rules the adoption of which (under certain circumstances) maximizes the good.

Global consequentialism: the moral quality of the evaluand in question is determined by its consequences.

demandingness problem   Act-consequentialism requires that we maximize the good, which collapses the distinction between a required act and a supererogatory one. This renders the theory demanding in that what most people regard as optional goodness becomes required by the theory.

global consequentialism   The view that the moral quality of anything is determined by its effects directly.

hedonism   The sole intrinsic good is pleasure; the sole intrinsic bad is pain.

indirection strategy   The strategy of determining the rightness of an action by appealing to effects, not of the action itself, but of something else associated with the action, such as a rule.

instrumental good   Good as a means to some other good. A *merely* instrumental good will not be intrinsically good.

intrinsic good   Good in and of itself.

local consequentialism   A form of consequentialism that restricts evaluation to a particular entity, such as an act or a rule.

moral absolutism   There are some actions that are wrong no matter the consequences.

normative (versus descriptive)   A normative claim is about what ought to or should be the case, in contrast to a descriptive claim, which is about what is the case.

objective consequentialism   The view that the moral quality of a feature of agency is determined by actual consequences.

persons actualism   The view that only the well-being of persons who actually exist or will exist has value.

possibilism   The view that the agent ought to consider what she *can* do in determining her best option.

repugnant conclusion   The conclusion that, if what we ought to do is maximize total utility, then it could turn out that the best state of affairs is one in which very large numbers of people live lives barely worth living, rather than the state of affairs in which a smaller group live much better lives.

scalar consequentialism   Moral quality judgments focus on 'better' and 'worse' rather than 'right' and 'wrong'; seen as solving the demandingness problem.

subjective consequentialism   Defines moral quality in terms of what the agent expects (or intends, etc.) to be brought about by her actions.

supererogatory   An action is supererogatory if it is good but not required, in the sense of going beyond what is required.

total consequentialism   The view that we ought to maximize total utility.

utilitarianism   The right action is the action that maximizes good consequences. Classical utilitarianism is further committed to the hedonistic theory of value.

NOTES

Chapter 1

1 *Letter to Menoceus*, in *The Essential Epicurus*, trans. and ed. Eugene O'Connor (Amherst, NY: Prometheus Books, 1993).

2 Geoffrey Scarre, *Utilitarianism* (London: Routledge, 1996), 27–33.

3 *The Ethical and Political Works of Mo Tzu*, trans. Yi-Pao Mei (London: Arthur Probsthain, 1929).

4 D. D. Raphael, ed., *The British Moralists* (Oxford: Clarendon Press, 1969), 412.

5 'Realism' and 'realist' are tricky. Given that Hume believed the moral perspective was corrected from a 'general' point of view, he is not, in my opinion, offering a subjective view. However, he does not believe that moral claims have a truth value beyond what is warranted by the normal, or usual, human reaction. So, in that sense, he is not a realist about morality. But in the sense that moral truth corresponds to something beyond the idiosyncratic agent's response, he is. I discuss this issue further in "Moral Sense and Sentimentalism," in *The Oxford Handbook of the History of Ethics*, ed. Roger Crisp (Oxford: Oxford University Press, forthcoming).

6 Raphael, ed., *British Moralists*, 188.

7 Lord Shaftesbury, *Inquiry Concerning Virtue or Merit*, Book I, part ii, section 3, in Raphael, ed., *British Moralists*, 173–4.

8 See Michael Gill, *The British Moralists on Human Nature and the Birth of Secular Ethics* (New York: Cambridge University Press, 2006).

9 Raphael, ed., *British Moralists*, 172

10 Joachim Hruschka notes, however, that it was Leibniz who first spelled out a utilitarian decision procedure. See Joachim Hruschka, "The Greatest Happiness Principle and Other Early German Anticipations of Utilitarian Theory," *Utilitas* 3 (1991), 165–77.

11 Raphael, ed., *British Moralists*, 283–4.

12 Scarre, *Utilitarianism*, 53–4.

13 Stephen Darwall, *Hume and the Invention of Utilitarianism* (University Park, PA: Penn State University Press, 1995), 216 ff.

14 Jeremy Bentham, *Introduction to the Principles of Morals and Legislation* (Oxford: Clarendon Press, 1907), 1.

15 Ibid.

16 J. B. Schneewind, "The Misfortunes of Virtue," *Ethics* 101 (1990), 42–63.

17 Jeremy Bentham, "Offenses against Oneself," ed. Louis Crompton, *Journal of Homosexuality* 3(4) (1978), 389–406; 4(1) (1978), 91–107; here 94.

18 Nancy Rosenblum, *Bentham's Theory of the Modern State* (New York: Cambridge University Press, 1978), 9.

19 For more on this see Wendy Donner, *The Liberal Self: John Stuart Mill's Moral and Political Philosophy* (Ithaca, NY: Cornell University Press, 1991).

20 John Stuart Mill, *Utilitarianism*, ed. Roger Crisp (New York: Oxford University Press, 1998), 81.

21 G. E. Moore, *Principia Ethica* (Amherst, NY: Prometheus Books, 1988), 66–7.

22 Mill, *Utilitarianism*, ch. 5.

23 See, for example, J. B. Schneewind, *Sidgwick's Ethics and Victorian Moral Philosophy* (Oxford: Clarendon Press, 1977).

24 Henry Sidgwick, *The Methods of Ethics* (Indianapolis, IN: Hackett Publishing Co., 1981), 490.

25 Bernard Williams. *Ethics and the Limits of Philosophy* (Cambridge, MA: Harvard University Press, 1985).

26 Sidgwick, *Methods of Ethics*, 415.

27 Derek Parfit, *Reasons and Persons* (Oxford: Oxford University Press, 1984).

28 Moore, *Principia Ethica*, 36.

29 Ibid., 189 ff.

30 Ibid., 199.

Chapter 2

1 J. J. C. Smart, in J. J. C. Smart and Bernard Williams, *Utilitarianism: For and Against* (New York: Cambridge University Press, 1973), 25.

2 Fred Feldman, "On the Intrinsic Value of Pleasures," in *Utilitarianism, Hedonism, and Desert* (New York: Cambridge University Press, 1997), 127–47.

3 Timothy Sprigge, *The Rational Foundation of Ethics* (London: Routledge & Kegan Paul, 1988).

4 Mill, *Utilitarianism*, 56.

5 Ibid.

6 I discuss the issue of false pleasures more thoroughly in "Pleasure as the Standard of Virtue in Hume's Moral Philosophy," *Pacific Philosophical Quarterly* 85 (2004), 173–94.

7 One recent development of hedonistic utilitarianism can be found in Torbjörn Tännsjö's *Hedonistic Utilitarianism* (Edinburgh: Edinburgh University Press, 1998).

8 Philip Pettit discusses this feature in his entry on "Desire," in *The Routledge Encyclopedia of Philosophy*, ed. Edward Craig (London: Taylor & Francis, 1998), vol. 3, 32.

9 Parfit, *Reasons and Persons*.

10 I discuss this kind of case further in "Memory, Desire, and Value in *Eternal Sunshine of the Spotless Mind*," in *Eternal Sunshine of the Spotless Mind*, ed. Christopher Grau (Abingdon: Routledge, 2009), 80–93.

11 Thomas Hurka, *Perfectionism* (New York: Oxford University Press, 1996).

12 Martha Nussbaum, *Women and Human Development: The Capabilities Approach* (Cambridge: Cambridge University Press, 2000).

13 I discuss this type of moralism in "Moralism," *Journal of Applied Philosophy* 20 (2005), 137–51.

14 Michael Slote, *Beyond Optimizing: A Study of Rational Choice* (Cambridge, MA: Harvard University Press, 1989), 157.

15 Gerd Gigerenzer, "Moral Intuition = Fast and Frugal Heuristics?" in *Moral Psychology*, vol. 2, *The Cognitive Science of Morality: Intuition and Diversity*, ed. Walter Sinnott-Armstrong (Cambridge, MA: MIT Press, 2008), 25.

16 David Goldstein and Gerd Gigerenzer, "Models of Ecological Rationality: The Recognition Heuristic," *Psychological Review* 109 (2002), 75–90.

17 Julia Driver and Don Loeb, "Moral Heuristics and Consequentialism: A Comment on Gigerenzer," in *Moral Psychology*, vol. 2, *The Cognitive Science of Morality*, ed. Sinnott-Armstrong, 31–40.

18 Don Loeb and I discuss this case, ibid.

19 Ben Bradley, "Against Satisficing Consequentialism," *Utilitas* 18 (2006), 97–108.

20 Mill, *Utilitarianism*, ch. 2.

21 Alastair Norcross, "The Scalar Approach to Utilitarianism," in *The Blackwell Guide to Mill's "Utilitarianism,"* ed. Henry West (Malden, MA: Blackwell, 2008), 220.

22 Elizabeth Anscombe, "Modern Moral Philosophy," *Philosophy* 33 (1958), 1–19.

23 Michael Slote, *From Morality to Virtue* (New York: Oxford University Press, 1995).

24 See, in particular, Schneewind, "Misfortunes of Virtue."

25 See, for example, Rosalind Hursthouse's account of right action in *On Virtue Ethics* (Oxford: Oxford University Press, 1999).

26 Michael Zimmerman, *Living with Uncertainty* (New York: Cambridge University Press, 2008), 120.

27 Jonathan Dancy, *Practical Reality* (New York: Oxford University Press, 2000).

28 Alastair Norcross, "Contextualism for Consequentialists," *Acta Analytica* 20 (2005), 85–6.

29 The interplay between these values is an extremely interesting topic in its own right. For further discussion, see Jeffrie G. Murphy and Jean Hampton, *Forgiveness and Mercy* (New York: Cambridge University Press, 1990).

30 J. R. Lucas, *Responsibility* (Oxford: Clarendon Press, 1993), 53.

31 Rosalind Hursthouse, *On Virtue Ethics* (New York: Oxford University Press, 1999).

32 Elie Wiesel, "The Perils of Indifference," speech given at the White House, April 12, 1999.

33 I discuss this issue, as well as the Williams negative responsibility view, in *Ethics: The Fundamentals* (Malden, MA: Blackwell, 2006), 71 ff.

34 H. L. A. Hart and Tony Honoré, *Causation in the Law* (New York: Oxford University Press, 1985).

35 Bernard Williams, in Smart and Williams, *Utilitarianism*, 117.

36 J. J. C. Smart, "Utilitarianism and Justice," *Journal of Chinese Philosophy* 5 (1978), 287–99; reprinted in *Utilitarianism and Its Critics*, ed. Jonathan Glover (New York: Macmillan, 1990), 170–4.

37 Timothy Chappell, "Integrity and Demandingness," *Ethical Theory and Moral Practice* 10 (2007), 258.

38 There is, of course, also the issue of what sense of 'can' is being employed in 'ought-implies-can'. In this characterization of the argument we assume 'psychologically can' rather than 'logically can' or 'physically can'. For example, Maria may physically be able to play chess since she is physically able to move the pieces in the right way, and yet psychologically unable since she doesn't know the rules of the game. We will return to this when we discuss criticisms of objective consequentialism later in the book.

39 Chappell, "Integrity and Demandingness," 259–60.

40 Lucas, *Responsibility*, 51.

41 Elizabeth Ashford, "Utilitarianism, Integrity, and Partiality," *Journal of Philosophy* 97 (2000), 435.

42 There is a wrinkle here, since 'good intention' is ambiguous between 'objectively good intention' and 'subjectively good intention'. For more on this issue see the discussion in Julia Driver, "The Virtues and Human Nature," in *How Should One Live?* ed. Roger Crisp (New York: Oxford University Press, 1996), 111–30.

Chapter 3

1 John Rawls, *A Theory of Justice* (Cambridge, MA: Harvard University Press, 1971), 26.

2 Ibid., 27.

3 Will Kymlicka, *Contemporary Political Philosophy* (Oxford: Oxford University Press, 1990), 31.

4 Parfit, *Reasons and Persons*, chs. 17 and 19.

5 Caspar Hare, "Voices from Another World: Must We Respect the Interests of People Who Do Not, and Will Never, Exist?" *Ethics* 117 (2007), 499.

6 Josh Parsons, "Axiological Actualism," *Australasian Journal of Philosophy* 80 (2002), 137–47.

7 Torbjörn Tännsjö, "Why We Ought to Accept the Repugnant Conclusion," *Utilitas* 14 (2002), 339–59.

8 Elder Shafir, Peter Diamond, and Amos Tversky, "Money Illusion," in *Choices, Values, and Frames*, ed. Daniel Kahneman and Amos Tversky (New York: Cambridge University Press, 2000), 335–55.

9 Ibid., 341.

10 See Amartya Sen, *Poverty and Famines* (Oxford: Oxford University Press, 1983), 39.

11 Samuel Scheffler argues for constraints and permissions with respect to good maximization in *The Rejection of Consequentialism* (Oxford: Clarendon Press, 1982).

12 Very many writers have made this criticism. The earliest version I am aware of appears in Sidgwick's *Methods of Ethics*, 257 ff. Most of these criticisms can be

avoided by objective consequentialism, which is compatible with the view that the value of friendship need not be *recognized*, or consciously thought of, as instrumental by the morally good agent. This is Peter Railton's line of response. Further, defenders such as Thomas Hurka point out that the criticism presupposes a non-teleological and, therefore, non-consequentialist, understanding of how one is to approach value – i.e. in terms of respect as well as promotion. The upshot is that the proper terms of the debate have to do with the attitudes appropriate towards value. See Thomas Hurka, "Value and Friendship: A More Subtle View," *Utilitas* 18 (2006), 323–42.

13 Frank Jackson, "Decision-Theoretic Consequentialism and the Nearest and Dearest Objection," *Ethics* 101 (1991), 461–82.

14 This is termed 'the cocktail party effect' and was first described by Colin Cherry, "Some Experiments on the Recognition of Speech, with One and with Two Ears," *Journal of the Acoustical Society of America* 25 (1953), 975–9.

15 Parfit refers to the version of consequentialism that allows for agent-neutral value as little 'c' consequentialism, in contrast to big 'C' Consequentialism, which holds that all value is neutral.

16 Jennie Louise, "Relativity of Value and the Consequentialist Umbrella," *Philosophical Quarterly* 54 (2004), 518–36.

17 There are some notable exceptions, including Amartya Sen and Douglas Portmore.

18 Matt Ridley, *The Origins of Virtue* (New York: Penguin Books, 1998), discusses the implications of the Wason test using experimental data provided by Leda Cosmides and John Tooby, 128 ff.

19 Robert Nozick, *Anarchy, State, and Utopia* (New York: Basic Books, 1974), 41. Nozick introduces this example in the context of discussing moral constraints with respect to animals. The analogy with people who view themselves as getting enough pleasure from consuming large numbers of animals to justify the loss of utility the animals suffer (that is, they are "utility devourers" with respect to animals).

20 Parfit, *Reasons and Persons*, 389.

21 Ibid.

22 Derek Parfit, "Equality or Priority?" The Lindley Lecture, University of Kansas, 1995.

23 Richard Arneson, "Luck Egalitarianism and Prioritarianism," *Ethics* 110 (2000), 340.

Chapter 4

1 See David Lyons, *Forms and Limits of Utilitarianism* (Oxford: Clarendon Press, 1965).

2 Brad Hooker, *Ideal Code, Real World* (New York: Oxford University Press, 2000), 32.

3 Ibid.

4 Ibid., 94.

5 Nick Zangwill, "Cordelia's Bond and Indirect Consequentialism," in *Oxford Studies in Normative Ethics*, vol. 1, ed. Mark Timmons (New York: Oxford University Press, forthcoming).

6 Hursthouse, *Virtue Ethics*.

7 See my discussion of this issue in "Virtue Theory," in *Contemporary Debates in Ethical Theory*, ed. James Dreier (Malden, MA: Blackwell, 2006), 113–24.

Chapter 5

1 Objective versions of consequentialism generally come in two flavors: those that define right actions in terms of actual consequences and those that define right actions in terms of objectively probable outcomes.

2 Moore, *Principia Ethica*, §17, p. 25.

3 Richard Brandt, "Toward a Credible Form of Utilitarianism," in *Morality and the Language of Conduct*, ed. H.-N. Castaneda and G. Nakhnikian (Detroit: Wayne State University Press, 1963), 107–43.

4 Niko Kolodny and John McFarlane, in "Ifs and Oughts," *Journal of Philosophy* (forthcoming), also note a nice observation made by Judith Thomson in support of the objective 'ought' and advice. Thomson notes that when she is asked for advice she does not believe that her job in providing advice is "limited to a study of what [she] believes is the case: I take it to be incumbent on me to find out what is the case."

5 Peter Railton, "Alienation, Consequentialism, and the Demands of Morality," *Philosophy & Public Affairs* 13 (1984), 134–71; reprinted in *Friendship: A Philosophical Reader*, ed. Neera Badhwar (Ithaca, NY: Cornell University Press), 211–44.

6 Bernard Williams, in Smart and Williams, *Utilitarianism*; Michael Stocker, "The Schizophrenia of Modern Ethical Theory," *Journal of Philosophy* 73 (1976), 453–66.

7 Sidgwick, *Methods of Ethics*, 413.

8 R. Eugene Bales, "Act Utilitarianism: Account of Right-Making Characteristics or Decision-Making Procedure?" *American Philosophical Quarterly* 8 (1971), 257–65.

9 Railton, "Alienation, Consequentialism," 233.

10 Neera Badhwar, "Introduction: The Nature and Significance of Friendship," in Badhwar, ed., *Friendship*, 28–29.

11 Railton, "Alienation, Consequentialism," 212.

12 Ibid., 226.

13 Ibid., 227.

14 Elinor Mason, "Can an Indirect Consequentialist Be a Real Friend?" *Ethics* 108 (1998), 386–93.

15 Paul Hurley, "Does Consequentialism Make Too Many Demands, or None at All?" *Ethics* 116 (2006), 680–706.

16 Ibid.

17 Dale Dorsey, "Weak Anti-Rationalism and the Demands of Morality," *Noûs* (forthcoming), develops such a view.

18 Hurley, "Does Consequentialism Make Too Many Demands," 705.

19 See the final chapter of Julia Driver, *Uneasy Virtue* (New York: Cambridge University Press, 2001).

20 Nomy Arpaly makes a case like this for Huckleberry Finn. See her *Unprincipled Virtue* (New York: Oxford University Press, 2003).

21 Joshua Greene and Jonathan Haidt, "How (and Where) Does Moral Judgment Work?" *Trends in Cognitive Sciences* 6 (2002), 517–23.

22 Ibid., 517.

23 See William Hirstein's *Brain Fiction: Self-Deception and the Riddle of Confabulation* (Cambridge, MA: MIT Press, 2004). For a discussion of 'provoked' confabulation

in healthy subjects, see M. D. Kopelman, "Two Types of Confabulation," *Journal of Neurology, Neurosurgery, and Psychiatry* 50 (1987), 1482–87.

24 Lisa Bortolotti and Rochelle E. Cox, "'Faultless' Ignorance: Strengths and Limitations of Epistemic Definitions of Confabulation," *Consciousness and Cognition* 18 (2009), 952–65.

25 Jonathan Bennett, "The Conscience of Huckleberry Finn," *Philosophy* 49 (1974), 123–34; Driver, *Uneasy Virtue*.

26 For an excellent account of why modern philosophy has focused more on action evaluation, see Schneewind, "Misfortunes of Virtue."

27 Alastair Norcross, "Consequentialism and the Unforeseeable Future," *Analysis* 50 (1990), 253–6.

28 Ian Hacking, "Possibility," *Philosophical Review* 76 (1967), 143–68.

29 Here, of course, we are not speaking of metaphysical possibility, but, rather, physical possibility.

30 Jackson, "Decision-Theoretic," 465.

31 Paul Horwich, *Probability and Evidence* (Cambridge: Cambridge University Press, 1982), 125–6.

32 Elinor Mason, "Consequentialism and the Ought-Implies-Can Principle," *American Philosophical Quarterly* 40 (2003), 321–2.

33 Feldman, *Utilitarianism, Hedonism, and Desert*, particularly the essay "World Utilitarianism," 17–35.

34 James Lenman, "Consequentialism and Cluelessness," *Philosophy & Public Affairs* 29 (2000), 242–70.

35 Thomas Nagel, "Moral Luck," in *Mortal Questions* (New York: Cambridge University Press, 1979), 25.

36 Adapted from Nagel's case, below.

37 Marcia Baron, "Remorse and Agent-Regret," *Midwest Studies in Philosophy* 13 (1988), 259–81.

38 I discuss this scenario, and what it means for responsibilities with respect to performing supererogatory actions, in much more detail in "The Ethics of Intervention," *Philosophy and Phenomenological Research* 57 (1997), 851–70.

39 Jackson, "Decision-Theoretic," 467.

40 Ibid.

41 Ibid., 465.

42 Jackson seems to have this view, and Gibbard mentions this as a position on the meaning of 'wrong'. Allan Gibbard, *Wise Choices, Apt Feelings* (New York: Cambridge University Press, 1990), 42.

43 See Frances Howard-Snyder "It's the Thought That Counts," *Utilitas* 17 (2005), 265–81.

44 William Frankena, "Obligation and Ability," in *Philosophical Analysis: A Collection of Essays*, ed. Max Black (London: Prentice-Hall, 1950), 148–65; Roy Sorensen, "Unknowable Obligations," *Utilitas* 7 (1995), 247–71.

Chapter 6

1 Bernard Williams, "Internal and External Reasons," in *Moral Luck* (New York: Cambridge University Press, 1981), 101–13.
2 Sidgwick, *Methods of Ethics*, 420–1.
3 Frank Jackson and Robert Pargetter, "Oughts, Options, and Actualism," *Philosophical Review* 95 (1986), 233.
4 Roger Crisp has pointed out to me that we could actually distinguish two further questions here – an agent-independent question and an agent-centered one. The first is the question of what one ought to do – the action that would or the action that could produce the best outcome? The second is the question of what one ought to do – ought one do what one believes will be best, or believes could be best? My take on this, to be argued for later, is that the actualism I favor be viewed as a realistic commitment on the part of the agent deliberating. So the focus is on the second question when it comes to discussions of agent deliberation.
5 Zimmerman, *Living with Uncertainty*, 120.
6 For a discussion of this consideration see R. H. Thomason, "Deontic Logic and the Role of Freedom in Moral Deliberation," in *New Studies in Deontic Logic*, ed. R. Hilpinen (Dordrecht: Reidel, 1981), 177–86.
7 Erik Carlson, *Consequentialism Reconsidered* (Dordrecht: Kluwer Academic Publishers, 1995), 127.
8 Jacob Ross raises this objection, echoing a blog post by Ralph Wedgwood (posted on PEA Soup, September 11, 2009), in "Actualism, Possibilism, and Beyond," in *Oxford Studies in Normative Ethics*, ed. Timmons.

Chapter 7

1 Williams, in Smart and Williams, *Utilitarianism*, 150.
2 Driver, *Uneasy Virtue*.
3 Parfit, *Reasons and Persons*, 24.
4 Philip Pettit and Michael Smith, "Global Consequentialism," in *Morality, Rules, and Consequences*, ed. Brad Hooker, Elinor Mason, and Dale Miller (Lanham, MD: Rowman & Littlefield, 2000), 121.
5 In "Fitting Attitudes for Consequentialists" (unpublished manuscript), Richard Yetter Chappell provides an alternative and novel rationale for why very expansive global consequentialism is mistaken. On his view, rather than centering on value, the consequentialist should consider 'fittingness' to be the basic concept in virtue of which we understand 'rightness'. On his view, value claims are understood as claims about what it is fitting to desire, and the latter notion is the more fundamental. The difference between actions and shampoo, then, is that in addition to asking whether it is fitting to desire a particular act, we can also ask if it is fitting itself, whereas we cannot do this with shampoo. This is a very interesting suggestion about how, in principle, to demarcate some types of evaluands from others.
6 Roger Crisp, "Utilitarianism and the Life of Virtue," *Philosophical Quarterly* 42 (1992), 139–60.

7 Michael Smith, "Consequentialism and the Nearest and Dearest Objection," in *Mind, Ethics, and Conditionals*, ed. Ian Ravenscroft (Oxford: Clarendon Press, 2010), 248–9.

8 Ibid.

9 Bart Streumer, "Can Consequentialism Cover Everything?" *Utilitas* 15 (2003), 237–47.

10 Parfit, *Reasons and Persons*, 32.

11 Campbell Brown criticizes Streumer for not considering the natural response of eliminating agglomeration. Streumer responds by admitting his argument relies on agglomeration, but that abandoning it does not save global consequentialism (or semi-global). Campbell Brown, "Blameless Wrongdoing and Agglomeration: A Reply to Streumer," *Utilitas* 17 (2005), 222–5.

12 Ibid., 224.

13 Robert Adams, "Motive Utilitarianism," *Journal of Philosophy* 73 (1976), 467–81.

14 Benjamin Franklin, *Autobiography*, ed. William B. Cairns (New York: Longmans, Green & Co., 1905), 38.

15 Earl Conee, "The Nature and Impossibility of Moral Perfection," *Philosophy and Phenomenological Research* 54 (1994), 815–25, presents this account and then criticizes it.

16 See Driver, *Uneasy Virtue*, chs. 1 and 2.

BIBLIOGRAPHY

Adams, Robert. "Motive Utilitarianism," *Journal of Philosophy* 73 (1976), 467–81.

Anscombe, Elizabeth. "Modern Moral Philosophy," *Philosophy* 33 (1958), 1–19.

Arneson, Richard. "Luck Egalitarianism and Prioritarianism," *Ethics* 110 (2000), 339–49.

Arpaly, Nomy. *Unprincipled Virtue* (New York: Oxford University Press, 2003).

Arrhenius, Gustaf, Jesper Ryberg, and Torbjörn Tännsjö, "The Repugnant Conclusion," in *The Stanford Encyclopedia of Philosophy* (Fall 2008 ed.), ed. E. Zalta. Online. Available HTTP: <http://plato.stanford.edu/archives/fall2008/entries/repugnant-conclusion/>.

Ashford, Elizabeth. "Utilitarianism, Integrity, and Partiality," *Journal of Philosophy* 97 (2000), 421–39.

Badhwar, Neera, "Introduction: The Nature and Significance of Friendship," in Badhwar, ed., *Friendship*, 1–38.

Badhwar, Neera, ed. *Friendship: A Philosophical Reader* (Ithaca, NY: Cornell University Press, 1993).

Bales, R. Eugene. "Act Utilitarianism: Account of Right-Making Characteristics or Decision-Making Procedure?" *American Philosophical Quarterly* 8 (1971), 257–65.

Baron, Marcia. "Remorse and Agent-Regret," *Midwest Studies in Philosophy* 13 (1988), 259–81.

Bennett, Jonathan. "The Conscience of Huckleberry Finn," *Philosophy* 49 (1974), 123–34.

Bentham, Jeremy. *Introduction to the Principles of Morals and Legislation* (Oxford: Clarendon Press, 1907).

—— "Offenses against Oneself," ed. Louis Crompton, *Journal of Homosexuality* 3(4) (1978), 389–406; 4(1) (1978), 91–107

Bortolotti, Lisa, and Rochelle E. Cox. "'Faultless' Ignorance: Strengths and Limitations of Epistemic Definitions of Confabulation," *Consciousness and Cognition* 18 (2009), 952–65.

Bradley, Ben. "Against Satisficing Consequentialism," *Utilitas* 18 (2006), 97–108.

Brandt, Richard. "Toward a Credible Form of Utilitarianism," in *Morality and the Language of Conduct*, ed. H.-N. Castaneda and G. Nakhnikian (Detroit: Wayne State University Press, 1963), 107–43.

Broome, John. *Weighing Goods* (New York: Oxford University Press, 1991).

—— *Weighing Lives* (New York: Oxford University Press, 2004).

Brown, Campbell. "Blameless Wrongdoing and Agglomeration: A Reply to Streumer," *Utilitas* 17 (2005), 222–5.

Carlson, Erik. "Consequentialism, Alternatives, and Actualism," *Philosophical Studies* 96 (1999), 253–68.

—— *Consequentialism Reconsidered* (Dordrecht: Kluwer Academic Publishers, 1995).

Chappell, Timothy. "Integrity and Demandingness," *Ethical Theory and Moral Practice* 10 (2007), 255–65.

Cherry, Colin. "Some Experiments on the Recognition of Speech, with One and with Two Ears," *Journal of the Acoustical Society of America* 25 (1953), 975–9.

Conee, Earl. "The Nature and Impossibility of Moral Perfection," *Philosophy and Phenomenological Research* 54 (1994), 815–25.

Crisp, Roger. "Utilitarianism and the Life of Virtue," *Philosophical Quarterly* 42 (1992), 139–60.

Dancy Jonathan. *Practical Reality* (New York: Oxford University Press, 2000).

Darwall, Stephen. *Hume and the Invention of Utilitarianism* (University Park, PA: Penn State University Press, 1995).

Donner, Wendy. *The Liberal Self: John Stuart Mill's Moral and Political Philosophy* (Ithaca, NY: Cornell University Press, 1991).

Dorsey, Dale. "Weak Anti-Rationalism and the Demands of Morality," *Noûs* (forthcoming).

Driver, Julia. "Dream Immorality," *Philosophy* 82 (2007), 5–22.

—— *Ethics: The Fundamentals* (Malden, MA: Blackwell, 2006).

—— "The Ethics of Intervention," *Philosophy and Phenomenological Research* 57 (1997), 851–70.

—— "Memory, Desire, and Value in *Eternal Sunshine of the Spotless Mind*," in *Eternal Sunshine of the Spotless Mind*, ed. Christopher Grau (New York: Routledge, 2009), 80–93.

—— "Moral Sense and Sentimentalism," in *The Oxford Handbook of the History of Ethics*, ed. Roger Crisp (Oxford: Oxford University Press, forthcoming).

Driver, Julia. "Moralism," *Journal of Applied Philosophy* 20 (2005), 137–51.

—— "Pleasure as the Standard of Virtue in Hume's Moral Philosophy," *Pacific Philosophical Quarterly* 85 (2004), 173–94.

—— *Uneasy Virtue* (New York: Cambridge University Press, 2001).

—— "Virtue Theory," in *Contemporary Debates in Moral Theory*, ed. James Dreier (Malden, MA: Blackwell, 2006), 113–23.

—— "The Virtues and Human Nature," in *How Should One Live?* ed. Roger Crisp (New York: Oxford University Press, 1996), 111–30.

Driver, Julia and Don Loeb. "Moral Heuristics and Consequentialism: A Comment on Gigerenzer," in *Moral Psychology*, vol. 2, *The Cognitive Science of Morality: Intuition and Diversity*, ed. Walter Sinnott-Armstrong (Cambridge, MA: MIT Press, 2008), 31–40.

Epicurus. *Letter to Menoceus*, in *The Essential Epicurus*, trans. and ed. Eugene O'Connor (Amherst, NY: Prometheus Books, 1993).

Feldman, Fred. "On the Intrinsic Value of Pleasures," in *Utilitarianism, Hedonism, and Desert* (New York: Cambridge University Press, 1997), 125–47.

—— "World Utilitarianism," in *Utilitarianism, Hedonism, and Desert*, 17–35.

Frankena, William. "Obligation and Ability," in *Philosophical Analysis: A Collection of Essays*, ed. Max Black (London: Prentice-Hall, 1950), 148–65.

Franklin, Benjamin. *Autobiography*, ed. William B. Cairns (New York: Longmans, Green & Co., 1905).

Gibbard, Allan. *Wise Choices, Apt Feelings* (New York: Cambridge University Press, 1990).

Gigerenzer, Gerd. "Moral Intuition = Fast and Frugal Heuristics?" in *Moral Psychology*, vol. 2, *The Cognitive Science of Morality: Intuition and Diversity*, ed. Walter Sinnott-Armstrong (Cambridge, MA: MIT Press, 2008), 1–26.

Gill, Michael. *The British Moralists on Human Nature and the Birth of Secular Ethics* (New York: Cambridge University Press, 2006).

Goldstein, David, and Gerd Gigerenzer. "Models of Ecological Rationality: The Recognition Heuristic," *Psychological Review* 109 (2002), 75–90.

Greene, Joshua and Jonathan Haidt. "How (and Where) Does Moral Judgment Work?" *Trends in Cognitive Sciences* 6 (2002), 517–23.

Hacking, Ian. "Possibility," *Philosophical Review* 76 (1967), 143–68.

Hare, Caspar. "Voices from Another World: Must We Respect the Interests of People Who Do Not, and Will Never, Exist?" *Ethics* 117 (2007), 498–523.

Hare, R. M. *Moral Thinking* (New York: Oxford University Press, 1981).

Hart, H. L. A., and Tony Honoré, *Causation in the Law* (New York: Oxford University Press, 1985).

Hirstein, William. *Brain Fiction: Self-Deception and the Riddle of Confabulation* (Cambridge, MA: MIT Press, 2004).

Hooker, Brad. *Ideal Code, Real World* (Oxford: Oxford University Press, 2000).

Horwich, Paul. *Probability and Evidence* (Cambridge: Cambridge University Press, 1982).

Howard-Snyder, Frances. "It's the Thought That Counts," *Utilitas* 17 (2005), 265–81.

—— "The Rejection of Objective Consequentialism," *Utilitas* 9 (1997), 241–8.

Hruschka, Joachim. "The Greatest Happiness Principle and Other Early German Anticipations of Utilitarian Theory," *Utilitas* 3 (1991), 165–77.

Hurka, Thomas. *Perfectionism* (New York: Oxford University Press, 1996).

—— "Value and Friendship: A More Subtle View," *Utilitas* 18 (2006), 323–42.

Hurley, Paul. , "Does Consequentialism Make Too Many Demands, or None at All?" *Ethics* 116 (2006), 680–706.

Hursthouse, Rosalind. *On Virtue Ethics* (Oxford: Oxford University Press, 1999).

Jackson, Frank. "Decision-Theoretic Consequentialism and the Nearest and Dearest Objection," *Ethics* 101 (1991), 461–82.

Jackson, Frank and Robert Pargetter. "Oughts, Options, and Actualism," *Philosophical Review* 95 (1986), 233–55.

Kagan, Shelly. *The Limits of Morality* (New York: Oxford University Press, 1989).

Kolodny, Niko and John McFarlane. "Ifs and Oughts," *Journal of Philosophy* (forthcoming).

Kopelman, M. D. "Two Types of Confabulation," *Journal of Neurology, Neurosurgery, and Psychiatry* 50 (1987), 1482–7.

Kymlicka, Will. *Contemporary Political Philosophy* (Oxford: Oxford University Press, 1990).

Lenman, James. "Consequentialism and Cluelessness," *Philosophy & Public Affairs* 29 (2000), 342–70.

Louise, Jennie. "Relativity of Value and the Consequentialist Umbrella," *Philosophical Quarterly* 54 (2004), 518–36.

Lucas, J. R. *Responsibility* (Oxford: Clarendon Press, 1993).

Lyons, David. *Forms and Limits of Utilitarianism* (Oxford: Clarendon Press, 1965).

Mason, Elinor. "Can an Indirect Consequentialist Be a Real Friend?" *Ethics* 108 (1998), 386–93.

—— "Consequentialism and the Ought-Implies-Can Principle," *American Philosophical Quarterly* 40 (2003), 319–31.

Mill, John Stuart. *Utilitarianism*, ed. Roger Crisp (New York: Oxford University Press 1998).

Mo Tzu. *The Ethical and Political Works of Mo Tzu*, trans. Yi-Pao Mei (London: Arthur Probsthain, 1929).

Moore, G. E. *Principia Ethica* (Amherst, NY: Prometheus Books, 1988).

Mulgan, Tim. *Future People* (New York: Oxford University Press, 2006).

Murphy, Jeffrie G. and Jean Hampton. *Forgiveness and Mercy* (New York: Cambridge University Press, 1990).

Nagel, Thomas. "Moral Luck," in *Mortal Questions* (New York: Cambridge University Press, 1979), 24–38.

Norcross, Alastair. "Consequentialism and the Unforeseeable Future," *Analysis* 50 (1990), 253–56.

—— "Contextualism for Consequentialists," *Acta Analytica* 20 (2005), 85–6.

—— "The Scalar Approach to Utilitarianism," in *The Blackwell Guide to Mill's "Utilitarianism,"* ed. Henry West (Malden, MA: Blackwell, 2008), 217–32.

Nozick, Robert. *Anarchy, State, and Utopia* (New York: Basic Books, 1974).

Nussbaum, Martha. *Women and Human Development: The Capabilities Approach* (Cambridge: Cambridge University Press 2000).

Parfit, Derek. "Equality or Priority?" The Lindley Lecture, University of Kansas, 1995.

—— *Reasons and Persons* (Oxford: Oxford University Press, 1984).

Parsons, Josh. "Axiological Actualism," *Australasian Journal of Philosophy* 80 (2002), 137–47.

Pettit, Philip. "Desire," in *The Routledge Encyclopedia of Philosophy*, ed. Edward Craig (London: Taylor & Francis, 1998), vol. 3, 32.

Pettit, Philip and Michael Smith. "Global Consequentialism," in *Morality, Rules, and Consequences*, ed. Brad Hooker, Elinor Mason, and Dale Miller (Lanham, MD: Rowman & Littlefield, 2000), 121–33.

Portmore, Douglas. *Commonsense Consequentialism* (New York: Oxford University Press, 2011).

Railton, Peter. "Alienation, Consequentialism, and the Demands of Morality," *Philosophy & Public Affairs* 13 (1984), 134–71; reprinted in *Friendship: A Philosophical Reader*, ed. Neera Badhwar (Ithaca, NY: Cornell University Press), 211–44.

Raphael, D. D., ed. *The British Moralists* (Oxford: Oxford University Press, 1969).

Rawls, John. *A Theory of Justice* (Cambridge, MA: Harvard University Press, 1971).

Ridley, Matt. *The Origins of Virtue* (New York: Penguin Books, 1998).

Rosenblum, Nancy. *Bentham's Theory of the Modern State* (New York: Cambridge University Press, 1978).

Ross, Jacob. "Actualism, Possibilism, and Beyond," in *Oxford Studies in Normative Ethics*, vol. 2, ed. Mark Timmons (New York: Oxford University Press, forthcoming).

Scarre, Geoffrey. *Utilitarianism* (London: Routledge, 1996).

Scheffler, Samuel. *The Rejection of Consequentialism* (Oxford: Clarendon Press, 1982).

Schneewind, J. B. "The Misfortunes of Virtue," *Ethics* 101 (1990), 42–63.

—— *Sidgwick's Ethics and Victorian Moral Philosophy* (Oxford: Clarendon Press, 1977).

Sen, Amartya. *Poverty and Famines* (Oxford: Oxford University Press, 1983).

Shafir, Eldar, Peter Diamond, and Amos Tversky. "Money Illusion," in *Choices, Values, and Frames*, ed. Daniel Kahneman and Amos Tversky (New York: Cambridge University Press, 2000), 335–55.

Sidgwick, Henry. *The Methods of Ethics* (Indianapolis, IN: Hackett Publishing Co., 1981).

Slote, Michael. *Beyond Optimizing: A Study of Rational Choice* (Cambridge, MA: Harvard University Press, 1989).

—— *From Morality to Virtue* (New York: Oxford University Press, 1995).

Smart, J. J. C. "Utilitarianism and Justice," *Journal of Chinese Philosophy* 5 (1978), 287–99; reprinted in *Utilitarianism and Its Critics*, ed. Jonathan Glover (New York: Macmillan, 1990), 170–4.

Smart, J. J. C. and Bernard Williams. *Utilitarianism: For and Against* (New York: Cambridge University Press, 1973).

Smith, Holly. "Culpable Ignorance," *Philosophical Review* 92 (1983), 543–71.

Smith, Michael. "Consequentialism and the Nearest and Dearest Objection," in *Mind, Ethics, and Conditionals*, ed. Ian Ravenscroft (Oxford: Clarendon Press, 2010), 237–65.

Sorensen, Roy. "Unknowable Obligations," *Utilitas* 7 (1995), 247–71.

Sprigge, Timothy. *The Rational Foundation of Ethics* (London: Routledge & Kegan Paul, 1988).

Stocker, Michael. "The Schizophrenia of Modern Ethical Theory," *Journal of Philosophy* 73 (1976), 453–66.

Streumer, Bart. "Can Consequentialism Cover Everything?" *Utilitas* 15 (2003), 237–47.

Sumner, Wayne. *Welfare, Happiness, and Ethics* (Oxford: Clarendon Press, 1996).

Tännsjö, Torbjörn. *Hedonistic Utilitarianism* (Edinburgh: Edinburgh University Press, 1998).

—— "Why We Ought to Accept the Repugnant Conclusion," *Utilitas* 14 (2002), 339–59.

Thomason, R. H. "Deontic Logic and the Role of Freedom in Moral Deliberation," in *New Studies in Deontic Logic*, ed. R. Hilpinen (Dordrecht: Reidel, 1981), 177–86.

Wiesel, Elie. "The Perils of Indifference," speech given at the White House, April 12, 1999.

Williams, Bernard. *Ethics and the Limits of Philosophy* (Cambridge, MA: Harvard University Press, 1985).

—— "Internal and External Reasons," in *Moral Luck* (New York: Cambridge University Press, 1981), 101–13.

Zangwill, Nick. "Cordelia's Bond and Indirect Consequentialism," in *Oxford Studies in Normative Ethics*, vol. 1, ed. Mark Timmons (New York: Oxford University Press, forthcoming).

Zimmerman, Michael. *Living with Uncertainty* (New York: Cambridge University Press, 2008).

INDEX

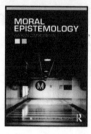